Read it Aloud!

A parent's guide to sharing books with young children

Monty Haas & Laurie Joy Haas

The Reading Railroad

Published by The Reading Railroad, 14 Woodland Street, Natick, MA 01760

Printed in the United States of America

Although the authors and publisher have exhaustively researched all sources to ensure the accuracy and completeness of the information contained in this book, we assume no responsibility for errors, inaccuracies, omissions, or any other inconsistency herein. Any slights against people or organizations are unintentional. Readers should consult educational experts for specific application to their homeschooling or individual training needs or requirements.

Library of Congress Cataloging-in-Publication Data

Haas, Monty.
    Read it Aloud!: a parent's guide to sharing books with young children/
by Monty Haas and Laurie Joy Haas.
      p. cm.
Includes Index.
Summary: Teaches adults how to bring books alive by developing read-aloud skills and character voices, and how to foster children's imagination, family communication, and reading readiness through interactive reading, wordplay, and reading and writing games.
    ISBN 0-9677400-0-2
    1. Reading. 2. Oral reading. 3. Parenting. 4. Family (books and reading).
    5. Reading – Parent participation. 6. Children – Books and reading.
    7. Reading games. I. Haas, Laurie Joy. II. Title.
649.58—dc21   99-091844

To Virgil & Florence Haas,
whose love made all of this possible

and to Patricia O'Brien, who believed in us and this book

You delight us with eye-opening ways to present literature to very young children and help us to understand that the love of reading and writing are keys to exploration, communication, and empowerment.

Director of resource and referral

TABLE OF CONTENTS

ACKNOWLEDGMENTS

When we reflect on those who have made this book complete, so many people come to mind. The first thanks, however, must go to our dear friend, Martha Lewis, whose love and research, and dedication to The Reading Railroad and its authors, put this book "on the right track."

Thanks also to Anna Whiteway for critiquing with creative wisdom— and to the entire Whiteway clan for providing children's writing samples.

For unflagging enthusiasm and "book savvy," thanks go to our friend and author, Jackie Greene, whose book-writing course is worth its weight in gold.

To Sharon Edwards and Robert Maloy, a special thanks for wrapping so many practical recommendations together with their refreshing brand of insuppressible joy.

We're especially grateful to James Gurney, whose love and exuberance both for reading aloud and our work has kept us excited, and fostered the concept of "setting the stage."

We are also greatly indebted to Jim Trelease, Amy Cohn, Susan Barrett, Barbara Bruce Williams, and Kim Kavanagh for helping us better understand how to reach those who will benefit from this book.

For the joyous and artistic look of our book, great thanks must go to Richard Bourque and Paula Wagner.

Our warm appreciation for regular encouragement, to both Jeffrey Levine and Kathy Kellett.

We'd also like to thank those who gave of their love, time, and professional skills to help us realize our goals: Elliott, Nancy, and Robin Reinert; Scott Laningham; Dave Casanave; Scott Martin; Karen Williams; and Larry Goeb.

Finally, our thanks to Dave and Jan Haas, Peter and Joyce Wills, Darrell Drummond, Dan Knowles, and David Anable.

I found [your ideas] opened up many areas of reading aloud that I had not thought about.

INTRODUCTION

As the 21st century bursts upon us, there are few areas of our lives that aren't affected by the technological changes that impact our world. Your children are growing into adulthood in a world glutted with mass communication. Interactive cable TV, the Net, cellular phones—a light-speed array of visual, aural, and written communication—demand and command their attention. What skills can you, as caring parents, help them build to meet the demands of this century? *The skills of communication.*

More conversation about what they see, hear, and are bombarded with daily will enable your children to think clearly when they're on their own. But having conversations that get to the issues can be challenging for families that have little time together and few precedents for open discussion. Where can those families get communication skills? With guidance, and more and more often the gift of books, many people are finding they can create a home environment where books are the springboard to a lifetime of communication.

Why is it important to share books? Not only does it give young children an introduction to the rhythm of language and build vocabulary, the very act of sharing a book introduces a topic for discussion and an opportunity for communication. Your children will be interested in reading books aloud and talking with you, even in an electronic age, if you value and understand how to make a place for sharing literature in your family. *Read it Aloud!* offers ideas and techniques that bring books into the center of the family circle, and that reflect our excitement about helping children learn to communicate.

We feel that by blending reading aloud, and in particular *performance reading*, with follow-up discussion, related activities, and plenty of word-play *today*, everyone can prepare their children to think, communicate, and succeed in their adult world *tomorrow*.

What is performance reading, and why is it important? Each time you read aloud to your children you're increasing their communication performance level. Coincidentally, their own interest in literature increases as you get comfortable performing more engaging and expressive reading techniques. So for us, *performance reading* means making an extra effort to benefit your children when you read.

Part I – Performance Reading teaches pulse-pounding, vibrant reading filled with dramatic involvement that fires your children's imagination and sparks their interest in the characters, the plot, the story, the book, or the poem. Through mastering performance reading skills you can ignite a love of reading aloud in your family.

Part II – Our Playful Language puts the whole family on speaking, writing, and laughing terms with what can seem to be the stuffy side of English! Through our **Win-Win Word Games**, you'll turn metaphors, spoonerisms, and other literary devices into friends that make travel time quality time, help you understand and share great literature, and lead to doing more creative writing.

Part III – Communication, Imagination, and Books is about establishing better communication within your family—while inspiring everyone to choose reading over the competition. You'll learn to tap into a book's information, imagination, art, and ideas in exciting ways that support reading readiness, imaginative play, family discussions, independent reading, and creative writing.

WHO CAN BENEFIT FROM THIS BOOK?

If you're a parent who is currently reading aloud to children, this book will act as a guide to using children's books and exploring ideas in ways that will strengthen communication within your family, enhance your reading time together, and lengthen it—not by minutes, but by years. If you have already stopped, we'll help you start again with wordplay and appropriate reading material in ways that comfortably build reading, writing, and oral communication skills.

If you're a parent-to-be, go ahead and jump right in. Although infants don't show a lot of response before reaching six months, we're amazed by reports of how much they take in—even prenatally! When the baby arrives, continue reading and honing your performance reading skills. You'll have begun a family tradition, a love of books, and the development of communication skills, right from the start.

If you're a homeschooling parent, use this book to teach your children performance reading skills and let them laugh as they learn to love literary devices. We've included both performance reading development exercises and word games for mixed ages or grades that will hold the interest of children of all ages while spawning a love of words, books, and communication.

If you're a new dad, we hope to help you develop a new and special bond with your infant-toddler that lasts a lifetime. Throughout the book we've included examples of the fun fathers have had learning and applying performance reading techniques.

If you're a caregiver, nanny, close friend, or visiting relative—you'll find concrete suggestions for sharing books and no muss, no fuss follow-up activities that'll grab kids' attention and help them learn to love literature!

If you're a reading volunteer—thank you. We'd like to help you as you share all the books, performance reading techniques, interactive reading ideas, and word games that you can with your own family, your schools, libraries, service club charities, and children's hospitals, where you are feeding our children's hungry minds.

WHY WE WROTE THIS BOOK

With this book we hope to spawn a revolution. A noisy revolution. A revolution of words and wordplay. Of ideas and shared conversation. Of books and imagination. We'd like to see more adults and kids reading together, talking, and getting excited as they share the creative ideas that grow out of their reading aloud. We hope that you'll use and share our ideas to help your children learn to listen carefully, analyze what is said, think about their decisions, communicate their feelings, and love those mind-stretching, creativity-sparking, awe-inspiring, life-defining resources called books.

ABOUT OUR GAMES

Each game is called a **Win-Win Word Game** for good reason. Children love to play noncompetitive, laughter-generating games with adults, and that's the only type you'll find in our book. Since there's usually a disparity among children's abilities, we prefer to build a sense of community and family while promoting a love of language. Everyone contributes as they are able—and everyone is a winner.

FOR MORE INFORMATION

For editorial comments (primarily ours) on resources mentioned in a chapter, see **Check it out!** at the chapter's end. The resources alone are listed in Appendix III.

ABOUT THE AUTHORS

The suggestions and ideas in this book are based on the authors' professional practice in the fields of broadcasting and education. For clarification of first-person references, specific examples reflect Monty's broadcasting and Laurie's experiences with children. You'll have to guess which of us was a television addict.

Laurie Joy Haas' talent for communicating with children in ways that inspire them to express their latent abilities has been the foundation for her success as a specialist in preschool, K–6, and afterschool programs.

This same talent of listening and fostering trust and communication with others has served her well as Laurie conducted interviews in the U.S., Ghana, Kenya, Nigeria, Switzerland, Germany, and England. These interviews went into a three-year, weekly, hour-long international radio program, which she helped to conceive, plan, and implement. Laurie worked alternately as producer and anchor.

Earlier in her lifelong writing and teaching career, Laurie crafted TV and radio campaigns as well as national magazine ads, catalogues, and brochures.

During this time Laurie developed and implemented a broadcast journalism course for a chain of broadcast vocational schools.

Monty Haas' career in radio spans the better part of three decades—most recently as a news anchor for WBUR-FM, the "all-news" National Public Radio affiliate in Boston. While serving as senior anchor/producer and writer for MonitoRadio in Boston, he hosted and reported for both daily and weekly public radio programs, which were broadcast coast-to-coast.

Monty was a writer and stringer for *Infoworld* weekly newsmagazine and has written bylined stories for *The Christian Science Monitor*.

As a Visiting Scholar in Mass Communications, Monty taught Radio and Television Announcing—a college course built on writing and public speaking. Additionally, he taught Video Practicum—which involved developing a weekly television news show; trained students in writing and presentational skills for television; and coached public speaking.

On the west coast Monty planned, wrote, and voiced TV and radio campaigns in the San Francisco Bay area and voiced industry films for, among others, Hewlett-Packard, Litton Industries, Racal-Vadic, and *Sunset* magazine.

Early on in his career Monty was program director for KBAY-FM in San Jose, California, and instructed at the Ron Bailie School of Broadcast teaching broadcast journalism, news, advertising copywriting, speech, radio history, and radio and TV interviewing.

Now that you have some background on the authors, hi! As co-owners of The Reading Railroad, we help parents communicate a love of books to their children. In addition to presenting workshops through organizations serving parents, educators, volunteer readers, and professional daycare and hospital staff, we write a monthly column, which is available at www.townonline.com. To find us, click on [Parent and Baby], then on [Ask the Expert], then on [Reading]. You may also wish to check out our website: reading-railroad.com. We'll keep you posted on any workshops or performance reading programs in your area. If you wish to talk with us directly, please call us on our toll-free number: 1-888-875-5368.

PART ONE

PERFORMANCE READING

The Reading Railroad

As someone who grew up hating reading, I find I spend more time reading to my children because I learned how entertaining it can be.

Assistant marketing coordinator, Mom

CHAPTER ONE

Starting with the Right Attitude

Many years ago when I was just getting into radio broadcasting, I had a program director who gave me some advice. I was young and thought it was unusual at the time, but he was absolutely right. He said, "Give 'em a smile, Monty, they can always hear a smile!" So I asked some of my faithful radio listeners if they could tell the difference. They could!

Try it yourself. Listen carefully to the radio. You'll not only hear smiles, but you'll be able to tell the mood of the announcer as well.

Similarly, if you're happy to be reading aloud because you and your children have so much fun together, you're sending this powerful message to your budding readers: Reading brings joy, fun, and excitement!

To increase that joy, we'd like you to try some techniques to make you completely *comfortable* and *proficient* at reading aloud to children of any age. You'll find skills to apply whether you're beginning with board books, which are printed on thick cardboard pages that little hands find easier to turn, picture books, or even fiction and nonfiction stories or magazine articles dealing with family members' interests and activities.

Your love, joy, and sense of excitement and fun can actually help to make up for what initially may be lacking in technique. However, as you continue to read aloud and build your skills, children will *get more out of* everything you read. You'll help your children to:

> listen,
> understand what's being said,
> feel the rhythm and pace of language,
> use their imagination,

follow a storyline,
anticipate and predict, and
connect with you and with books, the bearers of wonder and
     suspense.

How many techniques are there? Creative readers may add their own, but this part of Performance Reading presents each of the basic read-aloud skills, including:

getting comfortable with your voice,
breathing from the diaphragm,
varying your pitch,
slowing down,
using pauses effectively,
speaking clearly,
telling the story with your face,
becoming dramatically involved,
using character voices, and, particularly for men,
using your falsetto.

We've also included the skills of:

prereading and editing, and
setting the stage.

Don't expect to digest and master all of these techniques at once. Gradually work them into your reading with your children. Each time you apply a new technique, you'll improve. As you improve, you'll also relax and have more fun. Eventually you won't even think twice about your voice, but each time you read, your children will hear *not only* your *words*, but what you have to say!

PERFORMANCE READING PRACTICE
Establishing a comfortable general reading expression

RULES FOR 'THE SMILE DETECTIVE' (for all ages)
Sit back-to-back and take turns reciting nursery rhymes. Try to keep a straight face for all but one line—on that one, really smile and recite it as warmly as you can. The goal isn't to hide the line, but to be sure your partner has no trouble telling the difference when you smile. Once you've each heard *and felt* that difference several times, grab a book, cuddle up, and concentrate on keeping a slight smile as you read and enjoy the story. Your children will feel that added warmth and brightness.

'THE SMILE DETECTIVE' is an exercise to help you smile as you read aloud. Not a full-face smile that's uncomfortable to sustain, but a slight smile that expresses contentment and joy. If others have difficulty hearing your smile when you practice back-to-back, then turn up the heat—and warm it up a bit more.

I would highly recommend this to anyone who reads aloud to children.

Employee development specialist, Mom

CHAPTER TWO
Getting Comfortable with Your Voice

The human voice can create some of the most beautiful sounds in the world. Think of its beauty and power—it sings, soothes, calms, inspires, incites, angers, and laughs.

It can tenderize, harmonize, extemporize, and put a "smileinyorize." It can imitate animals, birds, rude noises (ask any twelve year old), machinery, musical instruments, weapons of war, your mother-in-law, your boss, your older brother, and your kid sister.

It can break your heart, shatter glass, wake you up, and put you to sleep.

Ahhh, the beauty of the human voice. But do you like yours? Probably not! Parents often don't like hearing their own voice as they read aloud to their children, and would never voluntarily read aloud to a group of adults. Most likely it sounds too high, too nasal, too weak, too thin, too breathy, or too soft. And you may find you even run out of breath.

Fortunately, there's an easy way to hear and isolate these problems and to start applying some simple techniques to remedy them. Begin by taping your voice on a cassette recorder and focusing on a single new technique.

You can record a story as you read it to your children; then later, you can listen to yourself, perhaps when you're together in the car. Children will benefit from the additional listening time and you'll hear how each technique you're practicing is coming along.

Don't be bashful or ashamed. Realize that even people with deep, rich voices are surprised and often disappointed to hear their recorded voices for the first time.

You see, in part we each hear our voice from inside our head, literally through the bone structure, which causes resonance that makes us sound lower to ourselves than we actually sound to others. So no matter how good the recording equipment, we are already in for a rude awakening. What may surprise your ear even more is a recording done on an inexpensive cassette player. Because it doesn't reproduce the full range of your voice, you don't hear the lower frequencies that really *are* a part of your voice. You may even think you sound like Alvin and the Chipmunks!

Of course there are times that your vocal pitch really *does* go up—usually when you're uncomfortable in front of a microphone or a group of people. Stage or mike fright tightens your throat and chest and has the tendency to cause shallow breathing. That same fear makes you close down your mouth and mumble! Add all this together and you can actually sound as though you're going through puberty again as your voice cracks and squeaks, your words tumble out and run into each other, and your enunciation drops to the level of a poor ventriloquist. Reading from whatever script, talk, or book with any or all of these stumbling blocks, *anyone* would be less than thrilled with the sound that comes out.

By improving your reading voice, you'll more comfortably read aloud with your children as you move together from board books and picture books into chapter books and novels. And of course, you can share these techniques with your grade school children who may already be facing school reports and microphones themselves! In the process, you'll get used to hearing your voice—and you may even start liking what you hear!

CHAPTER THREE

Breathing from Your Diaphragm

Growing up with a mom who felt that kids should mind their p's and q's, which included being kind and considerate of others, I was constantly being reminded to talk "in little voices." This was Mom's way of reminding her boisterous child that there's a time and a place for loud voices—outside on the playground—not around adults and certainly not inside.

Many children have big voices or enjoy talking loudly. After all, it's one of the few ways they can get a grownup's attention. When you're only two-and-a-half feet tall your voice makes up for your size.

In fact, have you ever wondered why babies don't *lose* their voices crying, and crying, and crying? Well, if even tiny babies can have such big voices, maybe we should take a minute to look at it! They utilize a technique you've most likely trained yourself not to use. It's called diaphragmatic (di-uh-frag-MAA-tic) breathing. Don't be put off by the name—it really helps with reading aloud. It can give you better voice control, variety, volume, and endurance. Sadly, most of us don't use the diaphragm muscle to support our voices. Often, we breathe from our chests in order to hold in our stomachs. But there's one position where breathing from the diaphragm automatically kicks in—when you're lying on your back.

So, to find out what breathing from the diaphragm is, try this: The next time you read to your child, stretch out on the couch, the bed or the floor. Hold the book over your head when you start to read aloud. Your voice is now using the column of air supported by your diaphragm and you'll find yourself less breathy and more relaxed. The pitch of your voice may even be lower now that you're breathing deeply. For a moment, set down what you're reading and place the tips of your fingers just below your ribcage. The muscle you feel is your diaphragm. Concentrate on feeling it supporting your breathing.

Reading in this position daily for ten or fifteen minutes as you read to your child, you'll slowly start to retrain yourself to breathe deeply whether lying down, sitting, or standing. As you regain the full support of your voice, you'll naturally become more comfortable reading aloud, and will have acquired a fundamental skill for performance reading. You'll even sing better! Nice, huh? Want to join your local opera company?

PERFORMANCE READING PRACTICE
Breathing

RULES FOR 'POWER BREATHING' (for all ages)

If you're accustomed to bedside reading, stretch out on the bed. If not, just stretch out on the floor and have your children sit beside you. Tell them you're going to play a breathing game while you read. Now, have everyone put one hand on his or her own diaphragm. That's the muscle just below the ribcage. Push your stomach out and fill your lungs with air. Feel the muscle expand? Now, purse your lips and start to blow. Flex the muscles in your abdomen and feel the support your diaphragm is giving your exhaling breath. Flex them again and feel the pulse of air coming out of your lips. Have your children do the same, and see how naturally they use the diaphragm, even sitting up. This takes a few attempts if you're unfamiliar with diaphragms—or if somebody's terribly ticklish.

Next, have everyone grab something to read. Make it lightweight (heft-wise that is, not necessarily in content!); you're going to be holding it over your faces and reading it aloud while lying on your backs. Now, taking turns, have everyone pick a page, take a single full breath, and begin reading aloud. See how far the breath takes you. Have the readers reread their passages sitting up to see which position works best for them. You may want to try this more than once to be sure you have your lungs as full as possible each time.

'POWER BREATHING' is really an important exercise to help you return to a natural breathing pattern. When you, like a trained singer, master diaphragmatic breathing, you will find that the increased support to your voice keeps you from awkwardly running out of breath. This technique is used in training broadcasters as well, which in part helps to give them that often-remarked-upon beautiful voice. That larger volume of air passing over your vocal chords gives you a richer, less breathy, more supported sound, while enabling you to read longer sentences more fluidly. Listen for the instant difference, and really concentrate on the expansion of the diaphragm so you can duplicate the action sitting up. Since you'd also like to be able to read with the same power when you're standing up at a podium or sitting around a table with your family, you'll want to practice on your back often—until you've trained yourself not to breathe shallowly from your chest again.

There is much more to reading aloud than just sitting down and reading through a book! I have demonstrated my new skills to many of my friends.

Volunteer reader

CHAPTER FOUR
Varying Your Pitch

Coming right on the heels of breathing correctly is working with your vocal pitch. The two are simple concepts but controlling both breathing and pitch takes practice. Unfortunately, when reading aloud most people stay with one monotone pitch, and as listeners we're bored to tears.

Most often, women and men have exactly the opposite challenge with pitch: women stay in their upper range, men in their lower range. Your "normal" range is the pitch you use for everyday conversation.

When you sing, you use your voice's range of pitch. Performance reading also demands that you use that range of pitch in order to bring reading aloud alive.

To begin, you may want to practice changing your pitch while you're stretched out for your breathing exercise. This will allow your diaphragm to support your lower and upper tones.

One way to become conscious of your range and to start working with variations of pitch involves humming. Try this: Take any simple children's book—with words—and open it up. Hum a low pitch to yourself. Now, change from humming to reading aloud at that same pitch. Try it for awhile until you're satisfied that you could easily switch to reading at that pitch without humming.

Now, hum in a slightly higher pitch and repeat the same exercise. Do this up and down the scale and you'll find yourself getting used to reading aloud using a range of pitches. If you're a man, generally spend more time getting used to your higher range, and if you're a woman, your lower.

Either way, once you realize the possibilities, you'll more comfortably switch pitches for voices as you're reading along.

Is that it? Not quite. In the last chapter you learned how to read aloud breathing from your diaphragm. The next step is to begin reading aloud from your diaphragm in a variety of pitches. Let's take a look at what happens when these two skills are combined.

To find out, start to read aloud, placing a hand on your diaphragm. If you're having a hard time finding it, place your hand high on your stomach.

Rapidly push in with your hand and out with your diaphragm to create a "wavering voice" effect. Add a change in pitch and you've already got the beginnings of some great performance reading voices! Once you're comfortable with diaphragmatic breathing, you'll be able to get the same effect without using your hand. Try a variety of pitches while interrupting your breathing in other ways as well—like coughing out your words, gasping for air, or noisily drawing in your breath. Each device will enhance any character voices you begin to develop.

We realize that this all may sound a bit complicated, like rubbing your head and patting your stomach at the same time, but as you continue trying out new breathing patterns when you read aloud to your children, they'll naturally become part of your repertoire. In later chapters you'll learn how to combine additional skills with controlling your breathing and pitch to fully create character voices, and to read with thrilling dramatic involvement.

CHAPTER FIVE

Slowing Down

It seems that everything we do in life we do in a hurry. And, if anything, the pace of life is getting faster year after year.

Even plain old reading aloud suffers greatly because of this speed-racer approach. The words, plots, characters, and storylines of books are crafted for provoking or informing thought, imagination, introspection, and discussion—not for speed. Ideas may come in a flash, but they often come after hours of contemplative thought. And, once they come they need to be explored. It takes time to try them on for size. Children's minds play with and enjoy new ideas the way their hands play with toys.

A book introduces new ideas, and thus is marvelously interactive as it prompts thought and spawns talk and discussion. But this doesn't happen at light speed—approximately 186,000 miles per second, or nearly 300,000 kilometers per second. So, when you pick up a book to read aloud, don't put on your track shoes … put on your slippers!

Most radio or television anchors or news reporters read in the range of 175 to 200 words a minute, covering approximately three-quarters of a full double-spaced page of type. That pace is fine for the news, in order to squeeze a lot of information into a short time allotment, but half that speed is closer to what you want when reading a children's book aloud.

How do you judge that? Easy. Just slow down until you think you're reading painfully slow—that's about the right speed!

Now, if you always read at a slow, deliberate pace without knowing how to *use that time effectively*, it can be boring, and painful to you and the listener. Instead, you need to learn how to fill that nice slow pace with the elements of *dramatic involvement* in order to bring in contrast— the sudden change, the darting figure, the sensation of speed. You can also develop your fullest and most playful voices as you read aloud more slowly.

A slower pace makes room for special effects too: For the haunting cry at night. The persistent tapping at the window. The drawn-out howl of the wolf.

The long-standing "King" of boxing, Muhammed Ali, made a clever statement that ties in perfectly with good performance reading, and specifically with the *pace* at which you read.

Before one of his famous bouts, he said he was going to "float like a butterfly, sting like a bee." Performance readers should adopt that concept. When the ideas you're reading warrant it, let your voice float so everyone has time to fully enjoy each image. At other times, with abrupt, uneven, noisy activity, make the sound of your voice staccato, sharp, abrasive—"sting like a bee."

In our next few chapters we'll give you the techniques to turn *boring or painfully slow* reading into *mysterious, suspenseful, humorous* and/or *beautiful* reading. As with perfecting the proper technique in breathing—from the diaphragm—finding a relaxed pace will take practice. It will come more easily as you focus on bringing out the full range of feelings, characters, and linguistic power of what you're reading.

Sharing a book aloud is like viewing a beautiful sunrise or sunset. Or eating your favorite dessert. You don't want to race through it to get it over with. You want to make it linger so you can appreciate its beauty and color—or enjoy its taste.

As you're painting pictures with your voice, your children are rediscovering their imaginations—and their love for books.

CHAPTER SIX

Using Pauses Effectively

Following close on the heels of slowing down are pausing and reading for the ear. Here's an excerpt to practice with—go ahead and read it aloud to yourself:

Black Beauty by Anna Sewell

The first place that I can well remember was a large pleasant meadow with a pond of clear water in it. Some shady trees leaned over it, and rushes and water-lilies grew at the deep end. Over the hedge on one side we looked into a ploughed field, and on the other we looked over a gate at our master's house, which stood by the roadside; at the top of the meadow was a plantation of fir trees, and at the bottom a running brook overhung by a steep bank.

Whilst I was young I lived upon my mother's milk, as I could not eat grass. In the day time I ran by her side, and at night I lay down close by her. When it was hot, we used to stand by the pond in the shade of the trees, and when it was cold, we had a nice warm shed near the plantation.

As soon as I was old enough to eat grass, my mother used to go out to work in the day time, and come back in the evening.

There were six young colts in the meadow besides me; they were older than I was; some were nearly as large as grown-up horses. I used to run with them, and had great fun; we used to gallop all together round and round the field, as hard as we could go. Sometimes we had rather rough play, for they would frequently bite and kick as well as gallop.

One day, when there was a good deal of kicking, my mother whinnied to me to come to her and then she said:

"I wish you to pay attention to what I am going to say to you. The colts who live here are very good colts, but they are cart-horse colts, and, of course, they have not learned manners. You have been well bred and well born; your father has a great name in these parts and your grandfather won the cup two years at the Newmarket races; your grandmother had the sweetest temper of any horse I ever knew, and I think you have never seen me kick or bite. I hope you will grow up gentle and good, and never learn bad ways; do your work with a good will, lift your feet up well when you trot, and never bite or kick even in play."

I have never forgotten my mother's advice; I knew she was a wise old horse, and our master thought a great deal of her. Her name was Duchess, but he often called her Pet.

All right, let's talk about what's going on here. First of all, throw out the notion that all commas, periods, and semicolons mean a pause. Those parts of sentence structure are necessary to help you as a reader *understand* what's written, but they can actually *get in the way* of the meaning for good performance reading. In other words, you need to do some beginning oral interpretation to bring out the meaning to your listeners.

If we pause, at, every, comma, as, we, read, aloud, we, would, bore, our, listeners, to, death! Reread this sentence where Black Beauty's mother is talking with him:

"The colts who live here are very good colts, but they are cart-horse colts, and, of course, they have not learned manners."

It's pretty choppy when you pause for each comma. A more logical reading would be for a short pause at the first comma, and no pause or a very short one after cart-horse colts. Try reading it in this more conversational way, and notice how much clearer the meaning is:

> "The colts who live here are very good colts ... but they are
> cart-horse colts, and of course they have not learned manners."

Depending on the text, even periods and other punctuation marks can be ignored or "downplayed" in performance reading. Try to think of what you're reading as *spoken* English instead of written English and you'll look for pauses that fit the ear not the eye. *This is a cardinal rule for performance readers.* Read for clarity, interest, and involvement, not for the punctuation marks.

Now, don't confuse fewer pauses in that sentence with picking up your speed. Keep your speed slow. Just remember not to pause at each visual cue.

This excerpt from *Black Beauty* is also a good place to talk about *painting mental pictures.* Another reason for slowing down your reading aloud and looking for variations in your pacing and for logical places to pause is to allow yourself the time for vocal expressions that paint the canvas of the imagination—yours, and your listeners'. Try reading this passage with a slow and languid tone:

> The first place that I can well remember was a large pleasant
> meadow with a pond of clear water in it. Some shady trees
> leaned over it, and rushes and water-lilies grew at the deep
> end. Over the hedge on one side we looked into a ploughed
> field, and on the other we looked over a gate at our master's
> house, which stood by the roadside; at the top of the meadow
> was a plantation of fir trees, and at the bottom a running
> brook overhung by a steep bank.

If you don't *see* what's taking place—the meadow and the pond and the surrounding shade trees and field—then you're just reading words.

In order to gather in your listeners, to take them on the same journey and share the same mental vistas, you need to slow down, look for, and find logical places to pause. Visualize for yourself not only the scenery, but also the feelings, joys, and disappointments of the characters, and the excitement, mystery, or tension of the plot.

Finally, when the action calls for it, don't be afraid of inserting a good … long … pause. You can really hook your listeners and hold them there for a few moments when the story gives you the opportunity. Try reading about the cart-horse colts as you've practiced, but introduce them with an attention-getting pause:

One day, when there was a good deal of kicking, my mother whinnied to me to come to her and then she said:
"I wish you to pay attention to what I am going to say to you.
(LONG PAUSE)
The colts who live here are very good colts, but they are cart-horse colts, and, of course, they have not learned manners."

Think where else a long pause would add to the power of what you're reading aloud:
> Before a loud noise in the text—a character banging on a door, a thunderclap or explosion.
> Before revealing *who done it* in a mystery story.
> After a very tender and gentle moment.
> After a harrowing chase scene.

Children will be thrilled with the suspense you add to stories!

CHAPTER SEVEN

Speaking Clearly

Try saying: "Unique New York" aloud, as fast as you can say it, at least five times!

We doubt you got it out clearly after number three, and you were probably laughing by then, too.

How about the old chestnuts—"She sells sea shells by the seashore," or "rubber baby buggy bumpers." Tongue twisters are wonderful for a number of reasons: First, kids love 'em. There's nothing boring about a good tongue twister. Second, kids and adults alike will accept the challenge and laugh at failure without feeling badly. But the third reason, and one that especially pleases us, is that tongue twisters can help you overcome mumbling.

This is a nation of mumblers, a killer when reading aloud, whether you're giving a speech, reading a position paper, talking at a club, or helping your child prepare an oral report for school.

We've had the opportunity to both observe and instruct in all applications of oral presentation: radio and television announcing, public speaking, acting, narrating, and performance reading. We're both active in the broadcast field, have critiqued our own recorded material, and have edited others'. We've come to this conclusion: No matter what kind of speech you're delivering or who you're speaking to, one of the quickest and easiest ways to immediately improve the sound of your voice—and the response of your audience—is to open your mouth and move your lips. *Exaggerate* your mouth and lip movements as you read aloud. We need to *over* compensate, because the norm seems to be *no* movement!

You have to work hard, moving tongue and lips much more than you normally do, to get through even the easiest of tongue twisters. A young friend of ours who spoke with a slight slur to her speech would recite several to us once a week. We found it helped her, and recommend them to you. Here are a few tongue twisters to try:

Three tree twigs
This is a zither
Six thick thistle sticks
Peggy Babcock
Toy boat
Unique New York

Mouth movements are the way you distinguish one sound you make from another as you speak. Articulation is merely being sure you make *all* of the changes. Have you realized how *we all naturally enunciate a bit more when we raise our voices to a shout in order for people to hear us?* We do … that's why "speaking up" helps. Speed, on the other hand, generally makes matters worse. We tend to skip a few mouth movements, and wind up stumbling through words. That's why slowing down helps.

To really master exaggerating your lip movements when you read will take a bit of practice. But that's not a bad thing. Years after you and your children have improved your enunciation, you'll both remember the fun you had digging up new tongue twisters, the ones you could never say, and the whoops of laughter you shared trying.

PERFORMANCE READING PRACTICE
Enunciation

RULES FOR 'HOMEMADE TONGUE TWISTERS' (for all ages)
Take a sheet of paper and write down two of the hardest tongue twisters you know. Or pull some from our list. To determine what mouth movements make them difficult to say, try rewriting them as nonsense tongue twisters based somewhat on their patterns. Then come up with some new ones. For example ...

"Three free thugs set three thugs free"

... can first become this nonsense twist that captures the difficulties:

"threep freep thuups set threep thuups freep"

... then new tongue twisters might be made that use some of the same tongue twisting elements:

"Tree frogs thaw 'til tree thaws freeze"
... or:
"Third flea thought she heard thoughts flee"

📖 📖 📖 📖 📖

'HOMEMADE TONGUE TWISTERS' are always the most fun when you come up with something that others can't easily say aloud. Often your first try at writing a tongue twister needs testing, then improving. By starting with "nonsense twists" you can first isolate the tricky sounds, then spend time later trying to come up with logical phrases.

RULES FOR 'TRICKY TWISTERS' (for all ages)
First, take turns trying to say these quickly, three to five times:

> Six slim saplings
> Six thin thistle sticks
>
> Swan swam over the sea,
> Swim, swan, swim!
> Swan swam back again,
> Well swum, swan!

Next, to understand what makes these particular words so difficult to say together, repeat one tongue-twister slowly, concentrating on the movements your lips and face must make to get the words out. Try to sort out the intricate changes going on inside your mouth. Now put your hand lightly across your mouth to feel the movement as you exaggerate each word, very slowly again. Practice saying your favorites over and over until you get them right, no matter how slowly. Then start speeding up gradually, until you can do them quickly and easily. HINT: If you start from a smile, you may find it easier to get the words right.

📖 📖 📖 📖

'TRICKY TWISTERS' helps you to feel your mouth and tongue working hard to distinguish sounds. It's also helpful to study someone else's face as she works with a tongue twister. When you've each practiced and watched the other practice, try having a conversation in which each of you continues to exaggerate your mouth movements. Try to carry some of this increased mouth action into your conversation with others. It may feel strange to *you* at first, but if you are the least bit natural about it, they will only notice how clearly you are speaking.

CHAPTER EIGHT

Telling the Story with Your Face

Now that you're breathing correctly, have slowed your speed and found ways to vary your pacing, have added pauses, and know you need to really move your lips, it's time to get the rest of your face involved in your reading! Your face is not only the key to fun, interesting, and good performance reading techniques, it's also the key to reading aloud with *different voices*.

We often think of kids as having "rubbery" faces. Perhaps you even grew up with a mom who said, "One day you'll be sorry you're making that silly face, because it'll freeze that way!" Poor mom, she was wrong. And now that's exactly what you want to keep in mind and start to practice when you're reading aloud—making those funny faces.

We need to come alive, to be animated and to feel involved in speaking or reading aloud. We must be able to smile, or frown—some children's stories demand a big frown now and then—or raise our eyebrows and open our mouths.

As adults most of us are terribly inhibited when we're doing any type of performing—presenting a paper or a talk, reading aloud from a book or play. When forced to speak extemporaneously in front of a group, we usually disappear behind a stiffened mask of a face with a tiny hole in the front through which a tinny, monotonous, unmodulated sound barely escapes. We're uncomfortable, and we don't look or sound natural. We don't even know *how* to look natural. So let's explore that a bit.

Under normal circumstances it's only natural to let your face carry its part of the message. When most of us are just casually talking or telling a story to a friend we tell it not only with our voice, but also with our face. Our face reflects what we're feeling, giving visual cues to the person we're talking with. Our features show joy, anger, disdain, sorrow, or surprise, which adds to our verbal message. Think about how you can surmise the tone of a conversation from thirty feet away just by watching the people's faces. Think how often actors don't need words. Mimes never do.

But to break the mask of fear and force your face to be involved in reading aloud takes a bit of practice on your part. Acting, if you will. So we've included some exercises that you can use to awaken your flexible features. Practice in front of a mirror *could* be helpful, but *not* if it just makes you more self-conscious. Instead, we suggest you practice with one of your children, mirroring each other's expressions.

First, raise your eyebrows. Really use your forehead muscles to pull them up toward the top of your head. If you're looking in a mirror, you'll see how that opens your eyes way up. Even if you don't, you can feel your eyes almost stretching. Where would a "face" like this be appropriate when you're reading aloud? It's great for showing surprise, innocence, youthfulness, and gullibility. And, believe it or not, your raised eyebrows will actually help you raise your vocal pitch.

Now that you've tried the "wide-eyed" look, let's practice its opposite. Squint your eyes. Force yourself to pull your eyebrows down and force your cheeks up in order to really "skrinch" your eyes together. Feel the muscles you use and the effort it takes to force your face into this shape.

Next, move from the squinty-eyed position to the wide-open position and back again. Regularly practice animating your face and thinking about what feelings and characters would lend themselves to these various expressions.

Now put these faces to work. What follows are two brief passages to read aloud to your child. The first is a children's poem that should be read with a sense of buoyancy and youthful joy. Keep your eyebrows pulled way up—which, you'll notice, helps you keep a lightness to your voice. Then picture your child, legs and arms pumping a swing, with you standing behind, rhythmically pushing. When you've got the beat, try the poem. The second passage, a version of Dickens' famous story, should be read with squinty eyes and a gravelly pitch to your voice—except for the last line!

The Swing
by Robert Louis Stevenson

How do you like to go up in a swing?
Up in the air so blue?
Oh, I do think it the pleasantest thing
Ever a child can do!

Up in the air and over the wall,
Till I can see so wide,
Rivers and trees and cattle and all
Over the countryside—

Till I look down on the garden green,
Down on the roof so brown—
Up in the air I go flying again,
Up in the air and down!

What you did with your face should have made a big difference in what your voice sounded like. Did you keep your eyes wide open? If so, did you hear the youthful innocence coming through? If not, record yourself reading the poem with and without the exaggerated open-eyed look so you can hear the difference for yourself.

In contrast, the squinty-eyed look would go well with a character who's crotchety or sneaky and secretive. Who else? Trolls, perhaps? Evil witches? Give it a try with *any kind* of sinister or spooky characters, and everyone will have some fun!

from A Christmas Carol
by Charles Dickens

Oh, but he was a tightfisted hand at the grindstone.
Scrooge! A squeezing, wrenching, grasping, scraping, clutch-
ing, covetous old sinner! Hard and sharp as flint, from which
hot steel had ever struck out generous fire; secret, and self-
contained, and solitary as an oyster.
"Bah" said Scrooge. "Humbug!"
"God bless us every one," said Tiny Tim, the last of all.

Now let's talk about what your "normal" at-rest face should be when
you're reading aloud. Keep in mind that your listener is looking for you
to set the tone. So, make sure that there's interest in your eyes, and a
slight smile on your lips. If you're having a good time, so will your
listeners. A blank, dull, or stony face telegraphs zero interest. Does this
really make a difference? Yes, indeed.

Now to be sure your general reading smile still leaves you room to
dramatize with a smile that rings with laughter, try reading this passage
aloud. It's about a young horse named Bunny and two of her young
mistresses. Keep it bright, but be sure you can still add an especially
warm smile when you read about the playfulness Laura was feeling:

from Bunny's First Bath
by Devon Whiteway

Bunny walked carefully to the edge of the creek, sniffed it,
tasted it, and finally touched it with her tiny hoof. She backed
up with a jerk. Mary cupped her hands, scooped up some cool
water, and gently poured it on Bunny's neck and forehead.
Bunny shivered. Laura scooped up some water too, but she
threw it all over Bunny and shouted, "Whee!!" Bunny bolted.
She splashed all around in the creek. She liked her first bath.

Did you have enough smiling room? And did you fill your face with surprise? Often, as in this case, the *narrative* holds the message of surprise or other emotion, rather than what someone is saying. So at those times you read the narrative with the expression on your face and the feeling behind the words. There are always many ways to read a sequence of events, but for now, try reading this passage again following a few more suggestions:

With a general reading SMILE:
> Bunny walked carefully to the edge of the creek, sniffed it, tasted it, and finally touched it with her tiny hoof.

With EYEBROWS UP IN SURPRISE:
> She backed up with a jerk.

With GENTLENESS:
> Mary cupped her hands, scooped up some cool water, and gently poured it on Bunny's neck and forehead.

With a SHIVERING motion:
> Bunny shivered.

SLOWLY, and more PLAYFULLY, with EMPHASIS implying SOMETHING is about to HAPPEN:
> *Laura* scooped up some water *too*,

Add a LONG PAUSE

With EYEBROWS UP IN SURPRISE, a CHUCKLE, and increasing VOLUME:
> [hee hee] but she *threw it all over Bunny* and shouted, *"Whee!!"*

QUICKLY—HARDLY PAUSING FOR THE PERIOD:
> Bunny bolted. She splashed all around in the creek.

Add a brief PAUSE before, then add EMPHASIS:
> She *liked* her first bath.

Feel the spirit of the moment? When you're able to relax and bring that memorable smile to your reading voice, feel the facial expressions and play with volume, add pauses and vary your pacing, your children will be able to picture and "experience" the events. They'll joyfully anticipate what's coming and love hearing every word. As for you, you'll have even more fun with the next step: getting dramatically involved!

PERFORMANCE READING PRACTICE
Getting your face involved

RULES FOR 'FACE SWAPPING' (for all ages)
Sitting in a circle or opposite one another, players raise and lower their eyebrows, making two exaggerated faces: the wide-eyed look and the squinty-eyed look. Exaggerate as much as possible by throwing faces (not pies) back and forth, reacting to each other.

📖📖📖📖

'FACE SWAPPING' can help you "loosen up" in order to more comfortably add facial expressions—and the vocal expression they bring—to your reading.

CHAPTER NINE
Becoming Dramatically Involved

There was a time in our nation's history when orators—eloquent public speakers—were taught their skills in public schools. People took pride not only in what they had to say, but *how* they said it. Today, some colleges and universities offer public speaking, or argumentation and debate courses, but the power of the spoken word generally has fallen prey to the sound bite.

Books are not newscasts and they shouldn't be read in the manner and style of the lead to a story on the nightly news. News anchors are obviously good readers but they aren't *dramatically involved performance readers*.

Dramatic involvement includes all of the techniques we've talked about so far and more. Dramatic involvement is, to the performance reader, what becoming the character is to the actor. When you see top performers in a play or film, and you fully believe that they really are the characters they are pretending to be, then they've achieved their goal. Likewise, when you're reading your children a book and they get completely wrapped up in the characters, the plot, and the fun and excitement of what they're hearing, then you know you've been dramatically involved with the book.

All the exercises we've outlined so far give you the building blocks to achieve dramatic involvement. What's next? You'll want to bring a conversational style and dramatic flair to your performance reading. By a conversational style we mean *involved* reading but not *affected* reading. What's the difference? Affected reading is self-conscious, stilted, stuffy or pompous—and hard to listen to. When, on the other hand, you're involved as a reader, you become a transparency for the unfolding story. In this conversational style, your heart becomes as engaged as your mind. You show emotions. You laugh, cry, giggle, smirk, purr, hiss, groan, shout, whisper—become *involved* with the *ideas*. Your children will love the excitement and get more out of what they're hearing. They'll better understand the emotions, reactions, and motives of the characters—and empathize with their dilemmas. The more real a story is to them, the more you'll have to discuss and share.

Now take this a step further: jump in, have fun, and heighten dramatic involvement by reading *in character voices!*

PERFORMANCE READING PRACTICE
Hearing your natural inflections

RULES FOR 'TABLE TALK' (for all ages)

Start a tape recorder near the telephone or dinner table before you talk to a friend or your family about something exciting in your day: maybe a funny incident with the kids or a fantastic sports play or an encounter with a long lost friend at the grocery store. Then forget about the fact that you're recording it! You want to sound as natural as possible.

Later, write out the story word for word, listening to your tone of voice, pauses, pitch, and volume. Note how animated your voice sounds, how it rises and falls with excitement and enthusiasm. When you think you can duplicate the expression of the original message, read and record the words onto the same tape, right after the first recording. Listen to one, then to the other. Is there a difference? Usually there is.

📖 📖 📖 📖

'TABLE TALK' demonstrates that when you're really wrapped up in the telling of an incident, you're sharing a moment in your life—you're not concentrating on words but on the story, on the *ideas*. With most attempts to read it back, that funny, engaging, exciting story sounds dull, flat, lifeless, and boring. Reading tends to come across as monotone when you're focusing on the *words*, which kills all liveliness. You must focus on the *ideas* when reading aloud to make words sound vibrant and alive.

I have started using voices and more animation in my reading aloud. It's more fun for my daughter.

Electrical engineer/ Dad

CHAPTER TEN
Using Character Voices

One of the most famous voices in the recording industry was the late, great Mel Blanc, the creator of the voices of Bugs Bunny, Daffy Duck, Elmer Fudd, Yosemite Sam, and a host of others. Reading a children's story aloud with dramatic involvement would have been no problem for him, but what about the rest of us ordinary folks?

You, too, have the ability to read with character voices.

You may not reach the level of a Mel Blanc, but your kids will be thrilled if you just try. And the more you try, the better you'll get. For the most part, if you want to attempt impersonations of characters that have already been given a voice by films or television, you need to develop a good "ear." You have to hear what makes one voice different from another and listen for distinguishing patterns. But even if you never can imitate Bugs Bunny or Donald Duck, you can develop simple character voices.

For example, there are numerous characters in children's stories who'll lend themselves to an Elmer Fudd-type voice. This is an easier voice than most, since basically all you need to do to reproduce it is slow your speed so you have time to first mentally then vocally turn all the "Rs" into "Ws."

"That wascally wabbit is going to wooin evwething!"

Now, since young children love it when you mix up something they're familiar with, apply that voice to a different type of character. You might, for example, use it softly for the voice of the Big Bad Wolf in *Little Red Riding Hood*:

"So, Wed Widing Hood, what did you bwing fo' Gwanma today?"

Keep in mind that voices are also tools to send messages. If you have a sensitive child, you can use this weaker-sounding voice to diminish the powerful image of evil. For an older child, using a weaker voice for an evil character may demonstrate how, at times, evil appears harmless—providing a great opportunity for discussion with your children.

Then there are those times you want to come across with an *attitude!* Forget what we practiced in an earlier chapter—opening your mouth wide and really enunciating—but only for this voice! Instead, almost close your mouth, clench your teeth and get ready for a great "bad guy" voice. Keep your teeth shut, just articulate with your lips and tongue, and once again add a bit of gravel to your voice. Ready to practice? Try reading the next three sentences aloud this way, starting now: If you can keep from laughing, you're on your way to another good voice. An additional helpful tip—squint your eyes as you read through clenched teeth. Put all that together, and you'll have a really great "baddy" voice that'll thrill kids.

A variation of this can give you different bad guys in the same story. From that clenched-teeth or only slightly open position, twist your lips to one side of your face and talk out of the side of your mouth. You'll have a different sound and a different voice to add to your growing repertoire.

Here's a voice that sounds like a thousand-year-old person. Force your lips out and around your upper and lower teeth. Now, talk, but keep your lips tightly wrapped. Grab a copy of *Hansel and Gretel* and have some fun reading the witch's part with this face.

We should say here that self-consciousness is going to threaten any attempts on your part to practice these techniques. As adults we've trained ourselves not to do those things that came so naturally to us as children. For some of us, exaggerating our expressions is hard enough. Really "screwing up" our faces and getting dramatically involved with a story may mean totally setting aside our adult definitions of ourselves—which can be tough to do. Still, you know the benefits, so kick that sense of embarrassment out of your thoughts and have some fun!

Naturally, you want to be able to use your character voices throughout a story. As you try different facial expressions, the voices that emerge will be character voices you can comfortably sustain. Working with *these* sounds, you might alter pitch and volume to come up with your variations. Remember a whisper can also be a voice.

You will have many choices, but sometimes it's more fun to give only one or two characters special voices. Not only is it easier for you to remember the voices from day to day, but those characters then really pop out from the crowd.

The more you use your new voices, the clearer they'll become and the more memorable they'll make the story—and its message.

PERFORMANCE READING PRACTICE
Applying facial expressions to character voices

RULES FOR 'SILLY ME' (for all ages)
Keeping in mind that facial expressions are the key to character voices, go to a mirror where you and your children can settle in for a voice and face-making session. Without using hands, take turns making exaggerated facial expressions. Use your shoulders, neck, and tilt of head to emphasize who or what you are—whether it's the motion of a slithering snake or the precise mechanical motion of a robot. Would an angry mouse look/sound the same as an angry bear? Would a surprised adult look/sound the same as a surprised child?

First identify yourself in character voice, then tell how you are feeling. Let your voice become charged with emotion as you do so. For example, when saying, "I am a FROG ...," can you add some tongue action? jumpy shoulders? bulging eyes looking for flying insects? Continue with a feeling, say, for example, arrogance: "... and I am very PROUD of my brand new feet." Can you express that pride with your eyebrows, the purse of your lips, and the tuck of your chin? Doing the gestures should enable you to come up with an appropriate tone of voice. Try varying the pitch to get contrasting voices: ("I am Ms. Frog ... I am Baby Sister Frog ... I am Uncle Frog ... and I am proud of MY feet too!). Then later, when you get to the story with the Mama, Papa, and Baby Bear voices, remember to change your posture and even the way your mouth opens. Play 'SILLY ME' often enough to get the feel of exaggerated differences of a variety of creatures and characters feeling ASTONISHED, PUZZLED, UPSET, SAD, CHEERFUL, and any other emotions you care to try.

📖 📖 📖 📖

'SILLY ME' will loosen you up for reading with expression, even with children you've been reading to for years. You might invite your children to play by announcing, "I feel SILLY—do you?" You may also be invited to play when you least expect it—or want it. If you must decline, try gently turning the invitation down in a character voice stating your own feelings at the time. A brief dialogue in character voices can be extremely satisfying to children.

CHAPTER ELEVEN
Using Your Falsetto

I grew up in a family that read aloud. Some of my best memories are of my dad reading aloud during family get-togethers. He had a beautiful voice and read aloud with great ease. I know that hearing him read influenced my appreciation for language, books, and the power and beauty of oral presentation.

For those of you who qualify as a male role model, *your* enthusiasm for reading and participation in reading aloud is critical. You can be the link between boys and literature. Your involvement moves reading off the list of Chores to the preferred list of Best Times with Dad. Sharing suspenseful, hilarious, thought-provoking books, you can make reading the equivalent of year-round summer vacation. Exploring the feelings and adventures of characters together, you can not only make personal connections with your children, but also turn them into lifetime readers.

Your bonus, as a male, is that you have the ability to produce a fun voice that most women can't. Because of the lower register or range of a man's voice, men have the ability to shift to a true falsetto. The beauty of this is that men are capable of sounding like Mickey Mouse!

To find your falsetto, start talking or hold a note and raise the pitch—not volume—of your voice higher than your regular speaking voice allows. You will feel a break point. Above that point lies a small creature voice, requiring only that you practice searching it out. One workshop participant, who apparently was *not* in a car pool, found it helpful to practice switching back and forth between voices on the way home from work. He'd make up a short dialogue to review the day's business or next day's appointments.

The look on kids' faces when a "serious" male adult starts talking like this is priceless—so cut loose! Again, put off any embarrassment you might feel, and realize how you can *delight* your children with yet another memorable voice, for the sake of literacy.

Some years ago one great dad was taking our workshop. Great, because he allowed himself to let go of being self-conscious and have some fun. He was away on a business trip and called home. His little girl answered the telephone. He instantly put on his falsetto voice saying hello and asking for mom. As he told us the story in class, with glee, his daughter put down the phone and exclaimed in wonder: "Mom! Mickey Mouse is on the phone!"

CHAPTER TWELVE
Prereading and Editing

Many years ago a piano teacher once told me that you don't really begin to learn how to play a piece of music until you memorize it. Your familiarity allows you to get beyond playing *notes* to playing *music*. The advice is also valid when it comes to reading children's books. Once you're familiar with a story and can apply the full spectrum of read-aloud skills, you'll help your children to catch all of the rhythm, ideas, and images that lie behind the written words.

But since there are so many different styles of writing, not to mention styles and stages of reading and listening, you will find that all books are not created equal. Simply put, sometimes even great books just don't lend themselves to *your* reading aloud to *your* children at a given time. If you hit a clunker, don't finish reading the text. If your kids aren't enjoying it, choose something else that you *both* like in order to keep that trio of joy, fun, and excitement in your performance reading.

Through experience and observation you will develop skill both in selecting and prereading books. You'll soon know if a book's "too old" for your child, or if it's not written for reading aloud: maybe there's no flow, no wordplay, no contrasts, or no rhythm. In that case, look at the pictures, start an illustration game, or simply pick another book.

Young children have short attention spans and will more easily take in short sentences, rhyming phrases, and immediately apparent plots. Older children who have not spent a lot of time with books may also have short attention spans. When reading beautiful books that stretch a child's listening ability, prereading can be especially helpful to you. You'll want to look through so that you are ready to engage them.

Actually there are many reasons to preread a story—even if you're just reading a chapter ahead in some books. For instance:

Choosing voices: Pitch is often used to distinguish characters by what they are (an elephant's voice is generally pitched lower than a bird's), but tone and manner of speaking can also be assigned, particularly to indicate traits or qualities. For example, laziness, arrogance, confidence, and nervousness can all be indicated with different voice patterns. Also, be sure to find out enough about your lead characters to figure out which is deserving of your wickedest laugh or your silliest faces.

Finding cliffhangers: If you serialize longer books, you'll want to build your children's anticipation of enjoyment by finding suspenseful stopping points.

Planning simple sound effects: Be ready to add a foot stomp, a knock at the door, a clap, etc., to enhance the story.

Dramatizing: Note which characters become excited and when to alter pace, pitch, and volume to add to the excitement.

Handling vocabulary (foreign and new): Don't let it stop you. If there's a pronunciation guide, practice a few times. When you're reading, do your best, and go on.

Finding opportunities for discussion: Familiarize yourself with where the story is going. Pick out major issues and decisions. Check them against the ending. Look for opportunities to address your children's personal losses or fears. Examine pictures and content for interactive reading possibilities; you can add our suggestions in Part Three to your own ideas.

Scanning ahead for smooth sailing: Get a feel for the spirit of what you'll be reading and see which character is saying what, and how. Unfortunately, even though you know the benefits, time often dictates that you can't closely preread a story, so you need to develop a scanning technique. It takes some practice but you can force your eyes to scan a few words ahead of what your mouth is reading. Soon you'll be able to quickly see where a story is going and "edit on the fly!"

Unless your children won't let you change the story because they've heard it before, you should be able to dodge most sticky situations. One word of caution, though. Scanning ahead doesn't always work! The classic and wonderful children's book *The Secret Garden* by Francis Hodgson Burnett was written in a style that defeats the scanning method. In this case, the author indicates the *way* a character is speaking far after the dialogue has started. So a passage that you've just "boomed" out may conclude with: "… she said quietly." There's nothing you can do about that if it happens, but laugh.

Determining appropriateness:

Humor and characters' relationships: Think of your children's maturity levels—how will they handle characters berating or hurting others? being sarcastic?

Emotional level: Don't read above a child's emotional level. Edit out inappropriate details, language, and gory spots. You know your kids. A particularly scary passage may be inappropriate for very young or sensitive children. Or, maybe you're reading just before bedtime and a frightening moment in the story would keep them awake. Edit it out. Tone it down. Take control.

Amount of narrative: Put a star in the margin to remind you to verbally edit excessive background description for young listeners—it can all be added back in later, when they're ready for it.

Plot: Everyone, including babies, feasts on books that beautifully present sights and sounds. But there comes a point when children need something more. As they take on the challenges of growing up, they enjoy and benefit from seeing characters face those same challenges in the books you share. Give them what they're ready for. Find books that reflect what's new and exciting in their lives. Are they beginning to notice cause and effect? Do they want to do some things without your help? Are they assuming new responsibilities? Reading a book that's filled with exciting and relevant information will propel them forward—in reading, and in life. Make it your business to search out plots you'd like to share. In Part Three of this book, we'll introduce you to several useful resources.

By taking the time to preread whenever you can, you'll be prepared to share more of what lies behind the words as you read aloud together.

CHAPTER THIRTEEN
Setting the Stage

The final step in getting dramatically involved through performance reading is creating an atmosphere of "specialness."

There's hardly a kid alive who doesn't love special occasions. Half the fun of anticipating birthdays, parties, Halloween, or the 4th of July is looking forward to the special things that symbolize those good times—balloons, cake and streamers, piñatas, candles, costumes and jack-o-lanterns, bands, parades, and special foods.

With reading aloud, what's most special to children is your presence. But their joy is heightened and their appetites are whetted if you find a way to draw attention to the fact that *you* consider your reading time together to be special.

A friend of ours, Jim Gurney, refers to this as "setting the stage." Jim has set the stage for his sons for years, along with writing and illustrating a best-selling series that includes *Dinotopia, Dinotopia: The World Beneath, and Dinotopia: First Flight*[1]—an innovative and fun combined book and board game. Think about how a theater production involves sets, costumes, rehearsed lines, and dimmed lights, all to give an audience the ability to suspend reality and go on a special journey. Kids have great imaginations. You don't have to do a *lot* to give them "a ticket to adventure," but do *something*! Make it simple.

You decide whether to cuddle in the old armchair and afghan, take a lantern to the tent or playhouse, hike into the woods, sit on the steps, or snuggle in bed with the stuffed animals. For special effects, dim all but your reading light. If it's summer, fire up the gas or propane lantern in the backyard or on the porch. Or light candles. For four nights in a row

Jim and his family had "Candlelight Evenings," a voluntary blackout. No electricity was allowed: no radios, no lights—not even night-lights. Their only exceptions were the furnace and the refrigerator. He found it lent a romantic atmosphere to their evenings, and especially to their readings, gathered in the circle of light around the kitchen table.

Jim also recommends having a special item of clothing to wear for your story times. He dons an old top hat. You could use an old silk scarf, pith helmet, baseball cap, or funny tie. You and your children are the set designers, stage managers, producers, directors, and stars of your show—so be creative, have fun, enjoy, and you'll all look forward to—and happily back on—sharing these special times together.

Check it Out!

1. James Gurney, *Dinotopia* (Atlanta: Turner Publishing, Inc., 1992); *Dinotopia: The World Beneath* (1995); and *Dinotopia: First Flight* (New York: HarperCollins Publishers, 1999). We might add that while the characterization of Dinotopian life is delightful fiction, Jim's skillful portrayal of prehistoric animal and plant life forms is all fact. His accuracy makes this series a popular addition to biology and botany curriculums for elementary school-aged children, and teachers often use his fictional world to enhance lessons on geography, as well. Don't miss taking your children to visit the official Dinotopia website <www.dinotopia.com>, one of the most popular sites for works of fantasy, and recognized as a Kid's Website of Yahooligans 1998.

CHAPTER FOURTEEN

Is That All I Need to Know?

One of the joys of reading children's books aloud is that you don't have to have a degree in oral interpretation to bring out the meaning in a clear, dramatically involved, conversational style. By practicing what we've covered so far, you and your children can reap many benefits from the books you share. But before we go on to wordplay and techniques for squeezing more value out of books, we'd like to give you a glimpse of why even professional speakers can have a challenge delivering the written word.

In fact, even many trained actors have a hard time getting their mouths, and thoughts, around the poetry, verse, words, and style of Shakespeare's writings or the King James Version of the *Bible*.

To read these aloud clearly, beautifully, and meaningfully takes a lot of study—both thoughtful analysis, and practice, practice, and more practice. Why? Because, as we've said, it's ideas you're reading, not words, and the message behind those words isn't as straightforward as in children's books.

If you've tried playing 'TABLE TALK' (p. 32), you know that even your *own words* can be a stumbling block if you're trying to read them aloud! Because of our background and work in broadcasting we've had to read from scripts throughout most of our careers. Learning to read your own script so that it doesn't sound "canned" is a challenge. This is why most written speeches sound as if they're being "read" when they're delivered. It takes a lot of practice to sound natural!

In our teacher training workshops we like to use a marvelously simple example to demonstrate how applying just *one* principle of oral interpretation can change the meaning of a sentence when reading aloud. This example is from a book that is no longer in print, *The Art of Reading Aloud* by John Dolman, Jr.:[2]

I am not going to New York this afternoon.

At first glance that statement seems to be so direct and unequivocal that it could hardly be misunderstood. But let us remember that our true thoughts are conveyed in vocal patterns, not in printed words alone. Variations in pitch, force, tempo, and tone quality profoundly change the meaning of the words, and with our four variables the possible combinations are almost infinite. Suppose for the moment, we consider only one of the four, namely force. Suppose further, we consider variations in only one kind of force: syllabic force, or accent. Let's see what happens to that simple sentence when we merely shift the main accent:

I am not going to New York this afternoon (though **you** may be).

I am **not** going to New York this afternoon (you must have mis-understood).

I **am not** going to New York this afternoon (and don't you say I **am**).

I am not **going** to New York this afternoon (I am already there).

I am not going **to** New York this afternoon (I am going **through** New York).

I am not going to **New** York this afternoon (but to York, **Pennsylvania**).

I am not going to New **York** this afternoon (but to New **Jersey**).

I am not going to **New York** this afternoon (I am going to **Washington**).

I am not going to New York **this** afternoon (perhaps some other afternoon).

I am not going to New York this **afternoon** (not till this **evening**).

Whew! And that's just with one simple change of force or emphasis when reading aloud. As you can see, the oral interpretation side of performance reading requires some "heavy lifting."

For those of you who wish to go beyond the scope of this book to develop your oral interpretation skills, we recommend a couple of books: *Speak for Yourself* by Jessica Somers Driver,[3] and *How to Speak the Written Word* by Nedra Newkirk Lamar.[4] These two will give you practical training and guidance. Neither of them is easy to find, however! So if you're interested and run into difficulty, give us a call or drop us an e-mail message, and we'll give you some additional sources.

Check it out!

2. John Dolman, Jr., *The Art of Reading Aloud* (New York: Harper & Brothers, 1956).
3. Jessica Somers Driver, *Speak for Yourself* (Jessica Somers Driver, 1948).
4. Nedra Newkirk Lamar, *How to Speak the Written Word* (Old Tappan, New Jersey: Fleming H. Revell Company, 1967).

You've given me the tools to work with my son for the next eighteen years.

Financial analyst, Mom

PART TWO

OUR PLAYFUL LANGUAGE

The Reading Railroad

I learned a lot [from your book] including that I shouldn't be so hard on my father for all that terrible punning. How was I to know that it was educational?

Public relations director

CHAPTER FIFTEEN
Introducing Wordplay

Now that you're eager to practice getting dramatically involved as you read aloud, is everyone ready to listen? If you've stopped reading aloud to any of your children, you'll first need to build some enthusiasm. By playing word games together regularly and mixing in light-hearted bits and snatches of reading to the whole family, you'll soon have the perfect environment for picking up a book or magazine to share longer stories, and more discussion and dialogue with your children.

The importance of this can hardly be overstated. Building communication bridges in the early years fosters trust, mutual understanding, and respect. Light-hearted wordplay opens the door to more serious or emotional discussion which good literature or life will bring up. A bond of sharing ideas, concerns, and fears creates an environment where even "hard" subjects can be brought up, talked about, and dealt with. And none of us—even your children—are exempt from the difficult subjects of violence, bullies, telling the truth, sex, and death. Start as early as you can to keep open dialogue alive and spontaneous in your family.

Where do you start? Pick up a child's joke book to read aloud. Even a simple "Knock, knock" joke that's a groaner to you can bring laughter, fun, and the joy of reading aloud back into your home. Maybe you remember this one:

> Knock, knock.
> Who's there?
> Dwayne.
> Dwayne who?
> Dwayne the tub,
> I'm dwowning!

Ask your young children if they knew that Roman citizens were very tiny people. When they say, "How tiny?" tell them about the Roman sentry who fell asleep on his watch! Corny? Yes. But often "silly" is the language of young children. They can't speak your language, but you can speak theirs. Choosing to read aloud simple jokes like these, or silly limericks for older children, gives your children a feel for language—and permission to laugh, share, and read back to *you* what pleases *them*. They'll soon see that **a pun is a play on words, sometimes on different senses of the same word and sometimes on the similar sense or sound of different words**—and they'll come up with plenty of their own. But as you groan, keep in mind that encouraging wordplay early on increases children's mental agility and gives them verbal tools and an appreciation for the power of words. Knowing how to use each literary device adds color, clarity, richness, and deeper meaning to everyday language, and helps your children acquire a taste for reading—and writing—well-written literature.

Mastery of our language and the ability to turn a phrase like a Shakespeare can begin with simple wordplay, word games, and banter. So let your home environment foster a love of language development where children can more easily become creative communicators.

Let them giggle over "gilly and soofy" *spoonerisms,* wrap their imaginations around shining metaphors, bowl you over with bad *puns,* and ...

rattle ... rattle ... slam! ... shudder ...

tap ... tap ... crack ... plop ...

sizzle ... scrape ... flip ... sizzle ... pop ... sputter ...

swoop ... scrape ... scoop ... plop ...

take you into the sound-effects kitchen with eggs *onomatopoeia!*

Soon your whole family will be kickin' around *similes* like a world-class soccer team!

CHAPTER SIXTEEN
Similes

Somewhere in the growing up phase, perhaps around eight to twelve years old, kids love to gross out adults and laugh with their friends with joyously juvenile *similes—comparisons constructed using the words "like" or "as."* For example …

> Your teeth are like stars … they come out at night.
> Your eyes are like pools … cesspools.
> Your lips are like cherries … they're the pits.
> Your face looks like a million bucks … all green and wrinkled.

You get the idea! In fact you might say, in kid-speak, that all of those examples are about as funny as a rubber crutch.

But don't despair just because those examples are about as nourishing and tasty as cotton candy. (Notice how we worked in that simile?!) Try these:

> Constant as the Northern star. —WILLIAM SHAKESPEARE
> Blue as the rain-washed forget-me-not. —J.R.R. TOLKIEN
> Fragrant as the breath of an angel. —OLIVER WENDELL HOLMES

Or these:

> Cruel as the crack of a whip. —MARGARET MITCHELL
> Mind like a sink. —AGATHA CHRISTIE
> Slept like a cocked pistol. —ÉMILE ZOLA

Similes paint pictures, fire the imagination, and play back in our thoughts like the refrain from a favorite song. How do you get from cotton candy to the Northern star? By using similes yourself!

When you're in a hurry, say "We have to fly like the wind!" or "Go quick like a bunny!" There are plenty of times to be "quiet as a mouse," and sometimes it helps to announce that you feel "prickly as a porcupine" and need to be left alone. As your children hear you using similes, they'll try them out and fit them into their own communications. Be sure to record some of the more descriptive similes your family comes up with.

Similies that are as precious as smiles:

_____

_____

_____

_____

_____

_____

_____

_____

_____

_____

_____

_____

Win-Win Word Games
Similes

RULES FOR 'FAST AS GREASED LIGHTNING' (for all ages)
Look around to find objects that could be classified as "straight as an arrow," "red as a beet," or would fit another familiar simile then announce the classification: "Let's find objects around us that are _____ as a _____." Everyone then looks around to see and call out objects that could fall into that classification. When no one sees any more, play passes to another observer, or you announce: "That was great—how many objects did we find that could be described as _____ as a _____?" Now let's find...." If you're in the car, your trip will go much faster, and your children will be pulling together to find similar objects. Or, so long as your prize dinner is not at risk, how about at the next meal start speaking to each other using a lot of similes! "These mashed potatoes are like drifted snow." "These bananas are as yellow as a toucan's beak."

'FAST AS GREASED LIGHTNING' may enlarge the vocabulary of very young children as older children help point out objects that are "crooked as a dog's hind leg" or "high as a kite." You may wish to move to "spongy" or "soggy," or other classifications that are appropriate, but for which you don't have a familiar simile. When you make up a simile for that classification, consider referencing a humorous shared experience, like "as soggy as (dog's name) was at the lake." Have children help you keep count. Variations will evolve, whether you think of things that are not visible around you, or just come up with humorous similes for objects that are. The goal is to have fun, and put appropriate ideas together.

RULES FOR 'DARK AS A MOONLESS NIGHT' (for all ages)
Each player tries to come up with a new simile that is scary. Each
time you play, the children themselves can throw out leads for the
group to think about:
As clammy as_____.
As cold as_____.
As gooey as_____.
As slimy as_____.
As squishy as_____.
Children manage to come up with plenty of these.

'DARK AS A MOONLESS NIGHT' puts to good use the intense interest children have in the unknown and spooky. Provide pen and
pad so children can write down their favorite phrases, if they so
choose, for future reference. Someone may decide to write a Halloween story, design a game, create a crossword puzzle—who knows!

CHAPTER SEVENTEEN
Alliteration

Kids always love the sound of *alliteration—a string of words in which several or all start with the same letter or sound.* Have fun repeating alliterative phrases aloud wherever you find them and point them out when you're reading aloud.

Here are a few lines from a book called *Great Gorilla Grins*: *An Abundance of Animal Alliterations*:[5]

> PENGUINS
> Prim penguins parade and pose
> in perfect pomp,
> puffed up with pride and importance.

Or, for a subject closer to home,

> PUSS
> Padding primly, puss patrols the parlor,
> She perches, purring, on plump pillows,
> peering and preening.
> Prowling among pantry platters,
> puss pilfers protein from her people's plates.

Then, in and around your days' activities, use alliteration to casually comment on whatever is happening: When *your* cat is making a speedy entrance into the room, announce: "Crazed cat comin' 'round the corner!" When it jumps up on your lap, let your children know you "feel furry feline feet!" On a walk through town you might stimulate alliterative exchanges by remarking, "I see cumulous clouds, tall trees, and straight sidewalks." Or you might ask an alliterative question: "Who can sing songs stepping sideways simultaneously?" The result will be that your children drink in more of the language, stretching for vocabulary they otherwise might ignore. You may even get to hear them come up with a few friendly furry-feet phrases on their own!

Our family's friendly furry-feet phrases, and other favorites:

_____

_____

_____

_____

_____

_____

_____

_____

_____

_____

_____

_____

_____

Win-Win Word Games
Alliteration

RULES FOR 'CUTE AND CUDDLY KITTENS' (for pre-K and K)
The group agrees upon a goal for the game: a number of words to be thought up starting with the same first letter or sound as an item pictured in a catalogue or magazine. A Counter is appointed, who counts out the total number in plastic game chips and puts them into a community stack. For each word given during play, the Counter removes a chip from the stack, keeping the game noncompetitive. At the beginning of every game, the youngest player selects and names an item, then says two or more random words that begin with the same *sound* as the item (For example: cat—cute, cuddly, cookie, kitchen). Working together, all players then name words until the stack is depleted. Dictionaries may be used if players are stumped before the stack is gone.

'CUTE AND CUDDLY KITTENS' may be started with several activities that develop small motor and reading readiness skills in young children: identifying and cutting out pictures together, pasting the pictures onto index cards, and writing names for objects onto the cards.

Older children may choose to add a qualifier to make the game more challenging for themselves, for example: the words they come up with need to be more than two syllables long.

To reinforce math skills without making a point of it, be sure to give the Counter time and permission to keep the chips in stacks for counting. You may occasionally ask how many more words are needed.

RULES FOR 'PARACHUTING PORCUPINES'
(for grade-schoolers)
Sitting in a circle, start a story using two words that begin with the same sound. The next person adds a new phrase having at least one word that repeats the same sound or having several that begin a new match. Continue around the circle making up a story as you go. As a variation, try having players repeat their parts of the story before the new person adds a part.

📖 📖 📖 📖

'PARACHUTING PORCUPINES' works for a group of mixed skill levels, giving everyone the opportunity to succeed simply by adding two words with the same initial sound. Children too young to conceptualize a story may be paired up with an adult who lets them volunteer one word, leaving the adult to come up with the alliterative match and the idea for the sentence.

RULES FOR 'SLAM DUNK' (for grade-schoolers)
Pick two words that start with different sounds (as in slam/dunk). The object of the game is to come up with an alliterative phrase using exactly eight words, most of which begin with either of the two initial sounds. For example, "Suddenly screamin' Sue stretched, slam-dunked, and delivered," or, (elves/tiptoe): "Early every evening, elusive elves tip-toe 'til twilight."

📖 📖 📖 📖

'SLAM DUNK' gets several people thinking together to solve a problem. They may all try to come up with the words, or one may choose to count words or write out ideas in progress. Try variations on the number of words.

RULES FOR 'SIDNEY SNAIL ESCAPES ESCARGOT'
(for grade-schoolers)
Try reading this sentence aloud with your children, then break it into alliterative phrases before translating into everyday English*:
Sidney snail, slowly and silently silvering steeples below big blue, paused to ponder, remembering randomly roaming reflective glass, gutters guarded by gawking gargoyles, and yes, in yesteryears, grass.

* Translation: Sidney Snail, slowly and silently leaving a silver trail on steeples under the sky, paused to think, remembering wandering across glass that reflected the light and heat, gutters guarded by bizarre statues of animals with their mouths hanging wide open, and yes, long ago, grass.

Now suggest everyone makes up his or her own escape story for Sidney!

📖 📖 📖 📖

'SIDNEY SNAIL ESCAPES ESCARGOT' has an inherent plot, with infinite possibilities for story development. A story could be started one day, and continued the next. Team writing could be fun, with Sidney's path taking many twists and turns. Once a simple alliterative phrase is thought up and praised, more are sure to follow. You may wish to start your own chapter book about Sidney's travels, with one or more illustrators. In any case, be sure to save the results on your original-story bookshelf, and read them aloud often.

Check it out!

5. Beth Hilgartner, *Great Gorilla Grins: An Abundance of Alliterations* (Boston: Little, Brown, 1979). You may also wish to look up books by Steven Kellogg, including *Aster Aardvark's Alphabet Adventures* (New York: Morrow, 1987); Maurice Sendak, *Alligators All Around: An Alphabet—An alligator jamboree with all letters, A through Z* (New York: HarperCollins, 1962); and Stan Berenstain, *The Berenstain Bears and Queenie's Crazy Crush* (New York: Random House, 1997).

CHAPTER EIGHTEEN
Metaphors

If you're lost in a jungle of meaningless words, drowning in a sea of alliterative drivel, and buried in a mudslide of confusion, don't be sad—you're just wrestling with the mighty metaphor.

Simply stated, *a metaphor is a word or phrase which relates two dissimilar things to give the reader or listener a bold, funny, moving, enlightening, or touching mental picture. It is often a short analogy.*

Metaphors are all around us. We use them constantly, but seldom stop to think about them.[6]

"The eagle has landed." —It's payday.
"She took the bull by the horns." —She confronted a hard issue.
"I'm in the doldrums." —I'm unhappy, lethargic.
"You got his goat." —You teased him until he reacted.
"They spilled the beans." —They told the truth about something.
"He went into a tailspin." —He became extremely despondent.

None of these can be taken literally. But figuratively speaking they spice up our language and generally illustrate how we feel about something.

Unlike similes, which are comparisons, metaphors are substitutions—leaving the reader to think about an author's implications. Our literature is full of metaphors: The clipper ship plowing the seas; or Shakespeare's "All the world's a stage"; or from Psalms, "If I take the wings of the morning."

This type of imagery is more than just colorful; it feeds the imagination with powerful images that ignite thought. Becoming familiar with metaphors, children will begin to understand and think more deeply about the ideas behind the words they hear and read.

The beauty of making up metaphors is that you can abbreviate what you're saying by calling on a familiar image to say it for you. It's a kind of shorthand. In his book *Loose Cannons and Red Herrings, a Book of Lost Metaphors*,[7] Robert Claiborne includes:

> The Lion's Share
> Everyone knows that this means nearly all of whatever is being shared out, but in the original version (or one of them) it was even more. As Æsop told the tale, the lion and three other animals went out to hunt. When it came time to share out the quarry, the lion divided it into four equal parts. The first he took as his share; the second, because he was king of the beasts; the third, for his mate and cubs—and as for the fourth, "let him who will dispute it with me!" The moral: don't go hunting with a lion.

Our language is full of such usages.

Metaphors can also be used to crisscross actions that are not normally attributed to certain animals or objects. This is a form of personification, or giving objects (or animals) human emotions or characteristics, like giving toes to stars:

> "Avast and ahoy, now adventure begins!
> Let's go to places where sharks show their fins!"
> They pulled anchor, set sail, and rallied about
> 'Til the sun sank down under and stars tiptoed out.[8]

Here's a poem that does just the opposite:

Smart Bomb
by Parker J. Whiteway (6th grade)

Effortlessly soaring high a half mile up
searching for a meal,
the Prairie Falcon stares down
seeing only flowing, waving grass.
Curling His wings in close
He drops like a bomb, homing in on a meadowlark
also looking for a tasty treat.
Again glancing down
the bomb corrects His trajectory,
a flick of His wings back out
and He's back on target.
The prey sees its attacker
and swiftly darts away,
the falcon opens His wings
and the chase is on.
No matter where it goes
the prey can't get away,
the falcon closes in
swiftly dodging trees.
Now over open fields
the meadowlark vainly beats its wings,
as the falcon with His lightening speed
crushes his prey with a single claw.
Four falconets impatiently scream
yearning for a meal,
in a moment their stomachs are filled
thanks to their father the smart bomb.

The subject is fraught with feeling, which is reinforced by the two metaphors, smart bomb and target. Even though the metaphor in the title prepares us for the inevitable, because we know a smart bomb will reach its target, we engage in the chase. Some readers will read as predator, having little concern for the prey, only admiring the falcon's moves. Other readers bring mixed feelings, accepting the inevitable while wishing life were different. The metaphors and their juxtaposition with those mixed feelings give this poem tremendous strength, making it memorable.

Point out colorful metaphors as you read books aloud. Start a journal of favorites with your children. Before you know it you'll see the fire in your children's eyes, then watch them illuminate their own writing and brighten your daily conversations with creative imagery!

Win-Win Word Game
Metaphors

RULES FOR 'LET'S TALK TURKEY' (for grade-schoolers)
First have everyone help make a list of animals with distinct characteristics:

  giraffe
  leopard
  frog

Add as many as you can.
Second, list the characteristics by themselves:

  long neck
  spots
  croaking

Now associate those characteristics with something or someone else:

  geese also have long necks

ripe bananas also have spots
poor singers croak

Finally, come up with a sentence or phrase that gives the reader a context in which to enjoy your metaphor, substituting the name of the animal for the similar person or object:

I guarded my lunch from the grabby giraffes of the pond.
She looked at the bananas: one leopard was crouching among the green.
She croaked out the words, but the tune was indecipherable.

As you can see, metaphors have a way of taking on personal, even judgmental feelings. Here are some that express mine. See if you can figure out what they're talking about:

I was lulled by the night's restful chorus.
I faced spring gardens choked with the litter of fall.

Did you guess? Those referred to my love for crickets, and my frustration each spring as I face the leaves that escaped raking in the fall.

Do a few together, then try to do some for each other without discussion to see how well your meaning comes across.

📖 📖 📖 📖

'LET'S TALK TURKEY' allows everyone to express both positive and negative associations or judgments with original colorful language. The fun lies in finding acceptable terms for expressing strong opinions, which we've all had from the time we first tasted strong foods.

Check it out!

6.   For an enjoyable guide to the origins of metaphors we hardly realize we use everyday, see the reference book by Robert Claiborne, *Loose Cannons & Red Herrings: A book of lost metaphors* (New York: Penguin Books, 1988). You might also look for a book by Robert A. Palmatier, *Speaking of Animals: a dictionary of animal metaphors* (Westport, CT: Greenwood Press, 1995).

7.   Robert Claiborne, *Loose Cannons & Red Herrings: A book of lost metaphors* (New York: Penguin Books, 1988).

8.   From the Laurie's unpublished collection.

CHAPTER NINETEEN

The Noisy Alphabet

One of the best alphabet books is *Chicka Chicka Boom Boom*[9] by Bill Martin, Jr., and John Archambault. We haven't met a single adult who doesn't instantly fall in love with the rhythm and cadence of this delightful book. Just 'cause you already *know* the alphabet, doesn't mean you won't want to read it aloud.

There are other ways to approach learning the alphabet and having fun. One we recommend is onomatopoeia—(ahna-matta-PEEYA). It's a funny word that means ... well ... here's what the *American Heritage Dictionary of the English Language,* Third Edition says: ***"Onomatopoeia: The formation or use of words that imitate the sounds associated with the objects they refer to."***

Or, in other words, *bark* is how we translate, or imitate what a dog says, while *boing* sounds more like a springy sound!

What follows is what we call "The Noisy Alphabet." It's not complete; we're missing a word for X—any suggestions? And, truthfully, we've stretched a bit on some of the others. But, forgive us. We were having too much fun.

One other thing. *You MUST read the list ALOUD!*

You'll miss too much of the fun

if you just read it quietly

to yourself ...

Ready?

THE NOISY ALPHABET

Ahem
Aiiiii
Babble
Bam
Bark
Beep
Biff
Bink
Blam
Boiiing
Boom
Boop
Bop
Burr
Buzz
Chickadee
Chirp
Chug
Click
Clink
Clop
Clump
Cockadoodledo
Crack
Crackle
Crash
Creak
Crinkle
Crunch
Cuckoo
Doiiing
Drip
Drizzle

Drop
Eek
Fizz
Gobble
Groan
Growl
Gurgle
Hiss
Honk
Hoot
Ick
Jangle
Jingle
Kerplop
Lub-dub
Meow
Murmur
Neigh
Oink
Oops
Peep
Ping
Pitter-patter
Plop
Pong
Poof
Pop
Pow
Quack
Rat-a-tat-tat
Rattle
Rip
Shutter
Skrinch
Skrunch

Sizzle
Slam
Slither
Slosh
Slurp
Snap
Splash
Splish
Sploosh
Sproing
Squawk
Squeak
Tap
Thump
Tinkle
Tweet
Ugh
Vroom
Whimper
Whir
Whoosh
Yap
Yay
Yelp
Yeow
Yikes
Zap
Zip
Zoom
Zounds
Zoweee

Smiling? Laughing? We are when we finish the list! We encourage you to make up your own noisy words, incorporate them in stories, and spring them on your kids whenever possible.

You and your children can make up your own sound effects-rich stories, or rewrite your favorites adding your own sound effects. Then record them to play back in the car when the whole family can learn the story with the sound effects and chime in together.

Write your first story's key onomatopoeia words here:

_____

_____

_____

_____

_____

_____

_____

_____

_____

_____

_____

_____

_____

Now write some or all of the Noisy Alphabet words onto individual cards, and you're ready to play our **Win-Win Word Games**.

Win-Win Word Games
Onomatopoeia

RULES FOR 'SPLISH, SPLASH, SPLOOSH' (for pre-K and K)
Have a child pick three Noisy Alphabet cards. You make up a brief adventure using the child's name and chosen Noisy Alphabet words. Your child may enjoy acting out the story as you go. For example, "Jamie said good-bye, patted the dragon's head, rushed to the water's edge, and 'sploosh,' disappeared across the sea on the back of a dolphin."

📖 📖 📖 📖

'SPLISH, SPLASH, SPLOOSH' invites you to personalize the sentences you make up for your young children. In so doing, you create an imaginary adventure specifically for each child, which you can make safe and exciting.

RULES FOR 'YIKES' (for pre-K and K)
Have your child turn over one Noisy Alphabet card at a time. You say the word, and let your child make up a sentence/story and act it out. Your child may choose to alternate with you as "imagineer"— or you may be drawn into the acting by his imagined scene. One scene can become a whole theme for play, all stemming from one word. Or, you can decide to select another word to bring new ideas into play. The key is to be flexible and imaginative.

📖 📖 📖 📖

'YIKES' allows the child to imagine his own circumstance; you merely do the reading and enjoy the show. *Note: Battles are often the TV-inspired theme. Death is often imagined, but hidden magical powers often resuscitate the victim. When you can, keep the violence down by making the battle some kind of a challenge: trying to free yourself from a sticky floor, crossing a raging river, or climbing a rocky mountain, etc.*

RULES FOR 'WHEE—OOPS—GROAN' (for grade-schoolers)
Deal three Noisy Alphabet cards to each player. Place the next card face up in the center, with the remaining cards face down in a stack. The first player uses both the word in the center and one or more from her own hand to start telling a story, discarding face up in a line as she goes. She replaces as many cards as she has discarded, then all players follow in turn, using one, two, or three onomatopoeic words from their hands to continue the story line. Players draw from visible discards or from the stack. Story may be concluded after each player has had three turns. Alternative endings may be offered by all players, using the cards in their hands.

'WHEE—OOPS—GROAN' is designed for the new reader as well as the more experienced. Of course you can always tell someone what his or her words say. But the reason you line up the words is so that anyone, notably a new reader who prefers to play independently, can pass over an indecipherable handful of cards for a word that has already been identified by someone else and used in the story. Repetition is often found to be humorous, so in addition to giving comfort and independence to the new reader, it can add smiles to the game. Sharing alternative endings allows everyone to be satisfied with the outcome.

RULES FOR 'ZOOM' (for all ages)
In a large group, have each player take one Noisy Alphabet card. Start the story, and let anyone jump in to continue the story line using his or her word. Tell non-readers their words.

'ZOOM' is simply a leveler, giving adults and children alike a way to be part of a whole, decide when to participate, and use their imaginations. Special events call for special themes, which the leader of the group can introduce. (For example: "The candles on the cake were lit, and Sarah was about to blow them out, when "whoosh," she, and the cake, and the candles were all blown into her favorite toy store.)

Check it out!

9.   Bill Martin, Jr., and John Archambault, *Chicka Chicka Boom Boom* (New York: Simon and Schuster, Inc., 1989). This is a great text for reading slowly, looking for each letter, having your child run her finger along the shapes of the letters, finding "loose-tooth T" and all the rest. It's also great to read it another time with rhythm—it has a bouncy feeling built right in. Encourage your little ones to listen carefully and chime in on the "Chicka Chicka Boom Boom" choruses.

CHAPTER TWENTY

Nyms

Most kids love "synonym" toast, and in fact, *homonyms (words that sound alike but have different spellings and meanings)*, *ant-onyms, (words that have opposite meanings), and synonyms (words that have the same meanings)* can be a wonderful source of fun, laughter, and vocabulary growth for younger children.

There are hundreds of homonyms in our language. While you may find it difficult to find them all in a list, they have a way of wheedling their way into a conversation—as puns! Introducing your kids to them early on—for example, by making up a *gripping tale* about a *gripping tail*—will give them a wonderfully fun way to build vocabulary and think about the interesting ways our language is put together. Here's a group of homonyms which can be used for some rainy day or car-trip fun.

HOMONYMS

Quarts—the measure
> Quartz—the crystal

Fur—animal skin
> Fir—tree

Flower—a blossom
> Flour—ground wheat or grain

Seas—an ocean
> Seize—to grab

Grays—neutral colors
> Graze—to feed on grass

Greece—a European country
Grease—cooking fat
Heard—hearing
Herd—a gathering
Sword—a long blade
Soared—flew
Tacks—small nails
Tax—a charge
Bear—the animal
Bare—not clothed
Assistance—help
Assistants —helpers
Awl—the tool
All—everyone or everything
Ark—a boat
Arc—part of a circle

What two-word homonyms can you add to the list?

_____

_____

_____

_____

_____

_____

_____

_____

_____

OK. Now that we've looked at some two-word homonyms, let's get into the real fun—three or more words. Can you think of any?

Frees—liberates
    Freeze—to harden with cold
        Frieze—a sculpted band
You—yourself
    Ewe—a sheep
        Yew—a tree
Cite—to present the facts
    Site—a place
        Sight—a view
Buy—to purchase
    By—at or near
        Bye—a farewell
Mail—posted letters
    Mail—armor
        Male—a man
Pair—a couple
    Pear—the fruit
        Pare—to peel
Rapped—struck quickly; performed spoken music
    Wrapped—covered over
        Rapt—fully engaged
Idle—not working
    Idol—an image
        Idyll—a poem
Cent—a coin
    Sent—past tense of to send
        Scent—an odor
I'll—I will
    Aisle—a passageway
        Isle—an island

What three-word homonyms can you add?

_____

_____

_____

_____

_____

_____

_____

_____

Any four-word homonyms?

_____

_____

_____

_____

_____

_____

_____

_____

_____

_____

_____

One final "nym" that is frequently used but seldom recognized is the *metonym*, which is ***a word involved in substitute naming***, or metonymy (me-TAHN-e-me). It may sound confusing but it's really very simple. Whenever you hear a Washington, DC, reporter say: *"The White House* stated today that ..."* you've heard a metonym. "The White House" is a metonym substituting for whoever actually said the words. A number of dictionaries use the example of "land belonging to the *crown.*" A more typical example would be to come home from work and say that "the *company* laid off a number of employees today." Or, that "the *service station* called and the car needs a new transmission." In each case you're employing a figure of speech. The *White House* can't really talk and the *service station* will never call.

Do we hear you asking: Why is it important to know that? I've been reading, writing, and speaking for (fill in the blank) years and I've gotten along fine without knowing about metonyms.

True!

But, as we've said, children's minds are thirsty. They'll soak up anything and everything. Showing them the "inner workings" of our language in a fun way, early on, can give them a love of words and a mastery of the English language, which they'll carry with them down whatever path of life they choose.

Win-Win Word Game
Homonyms and puns

RULES FOR 'PUN PICTURES' (for grade-schoolers)
With your children, use blank index cards and colorful nontoxic markers to make homonym cards; use drawing paper for pun pictures:

Each card has two homonyms, one on each side.
Side one might look like this:

(picture of a fir tree)   This is a f-i-r tree.
                            What is spelled f-u-r?

(Side two, then, has a picture of a fox)
                            This fox is covered with f-u-r.
                            What is spelled f-i-r?

Additional examples:
(picture of a flower)   This is a f-l-o-w-e-r.
                            What is spelled f-l-o-u-r?

(picture of grain and flour sack)
                            Grains and wheat are ground into f-l-o-u-r.
                            What is spelled f-l-o-w-e-r?

(picture of letter)   This is a piece of m-a-i-l.
                            What is spelled m-a-l-e?

(picture of universal symbols used to designate male)
                            These are universal symbols for m-a-l-e.
                            What is spelled m-a-i-l?

Once the cards are made, check them over by reading both sides of each card aloud. Correct any misspellings. Then ask if any player knows how a pun works. If you need to give a hint, choose a card and ask a leading question. For example, ask if anybody can draw what a mountain covered with F-U-R would look like.

📖 📖 📖 📖 📖

'PUN PICTURES' is for individual or group practice in recognizing and spelling homonyms—and making up puns! When introducing the game, match vocabulary to age of players. More advanced players may choose their own words from the list, using two of three homonyms as necessary. Have plenty of drawing paper nearby to make a book of puns. *Be sure finished illustrations are correctly labeled.*

Win-Win Word Game
Homonyms

RULES FOR 'CITING THE SIGHTS' (for upper grade-schoolers)
Using a homonym in a sentence, begin a story. Another player then continues the story with a sentence using a matching homonym, and introducing another new homonym. The next player can match either the first or second homonym, or both, and may add yet another homonym. Repeats are allowed, and players may pick up missed matches at any time. Notice s-e-n-t/*c-e-n-t*/*s-c-e-n-t* in the following example, as well as r-i-g-h-t/*w-r-i-t-e* and m-a-i-l/*m-a-l-e*:

Begin:
> "Tony *s-e-n-t* a letter to his brother today."

(Response #1 matches the homonym and introduces a second):
> "He licked a 32-*c-e-n-t* stamp and placed it on the r-i-g-h-t front corner of the letter."

(Response #2 matches either of the homonyms or both, and may add yet another. In this case, a match is made to the second homonym, and the player adds a third):
> "Tony doesn't *w-r-i-t-e* often, so he doesn't get much m-a-i-l."

(Response #3 picks up on any homonyms in play, and may introduce another. In this case the player picks up on an old match):
> "Once a *m-a-l-e* friend of his received a letter that had a *s-c-e-n-t*."

And so on. See how long you can go before having to start again.

📖 📖 📖 📖

'CITING THE SIGHTS' is for any number of players, all of whom will need a working knowledge of homonyms. You may begin playing with a copy of our list, and any words you wish to add, out on the table. When someone is stumped as to options for a response, make the list available as a reference sheet without attaching any penalty. It's good for children to look up the information they need.

Win-Win Word Game
Synonyms

RULES FOR 'I'M COOKING THE SAURUS ITS SUPPER'
(for all ages)

A player begins with the opening statement, "I'm cooking the saurus its supper so I'm ... warming words in the wok." The player then says, "I think the ducks (or another choice of animals) are hungry." Another player responds, "I'm cooking the *ducks* their supper so I'm ..." That player then chooses a cooking synonym to go with duck food like, "... sautéing snails in slime." Or they may ask, "What do ducks eat?" at which point there may be a quick discussion or, if no one really knows, a look-up in the encyclopedia to discover that they eat duckweed and snails, among other things. With that knowledge, that player might just as easily have come up with "... so I'm dicing duckweed." That player then suggests that another animal may be hungry, and so it continues back and forth from player to player:

"I think the cows are hungry!"
"I'm cooking the *cows* their supper so I'm ... braising bales of

hay. I think the rabbits are hungry!"
"I'm cooking the rabbits their supper so I'm … cutting up carrots."

You can use any cooking or food preparation terms you can think of, with or without using alliteration. Here's a list of synonyms to help any player who'd like to match the beginning sounds:

> add, bake, beat, boil, broil, brown, burn, chafe, char, cut, dice, dip, fill, glaze, heat, julienne, knead, marinate, melt, mix, par boil, pare, parch, peel, pickle, pour, remove, rinse, roast, roll, sauté, scorch, sear, simmer, singe, slice, smoke, steam, stew, stir, toss, toast, warm, whip.

'I'M COOKING THE SAURUS ITS SUPPER' helps children see how many different words can fall together as one set of synonyms. You may wish to look up "cooking" in a thesaurus so they can see how a thesaurus is set up and what a great help it can be. If your thesaurus has an index it will send you to the list of words that relate to your subject. Once you've found the synonyms, you may wish to look up one of *those* words. (If they're highlighted, it means they're also in the index.) You're effectively paring down the set of synonyms to get to a particular shade of meaning. Computer users may type in a word from our list, highlight it, and choose thesaurus from the software's writing tools to find more sets of related words.

Win-Win Word Game

Antonyms

RULES FOR 'ALIEN PLANET' (for grade-schoolers)

You have arrived on a new planet, where every object you see is familiar, but different. Starting with tangible descriptive words, for example, "big" and "little," "light and heavy," "tall and short," "large and small," "hard and soft," and other common pairs of *physical* opposites, have each player close her eyes and describe as many pairs of objects as she can that have switched descriptive words. For example, "I see huge gumdrops and tiny cakes on the table."

Gradually try more complex opposites—perhaps describing something about the planet's alien beings: what they do "inside and outside" (using *directional* opposites); what sounds they make that are "loud and soft" (using *relative* terms as opposed to the tangible pair "*hard* and soft"); and how they feel about what they do (using *emotional* terms like "calm and excited"). For example, "Aliens get very excited pulling weeds and are calm at baseball games."

'ALIEN PLANET' introduces possibilities that are quite humorous to preschoolers and kindergartners while helping to clarify language that may still be somewhat confusing. List antonyms you plan to suggest before you begin to play with children. Here are a few more:
    black/white, light/dark, up/down, in/out, here/there,
    fast/slow, go/come, buy/sell, give/take, raise/lower,
    whisper/shout.

CHAPTER TWENTY-ONE
Go Ghoti

The English language has some of the funniest spellings and pronunciations in the world. If it's your mother tongue, be grateful! It's tough to learn.

In fact, take the word "tough." As we all know, it's pronounced TUFF. Using logic we'd have little trouble sounding out "enough," and "rough." But what about "dough"? It's not pronounced DUFF, but DOE.

Some words change in pronunciation from their singular form to their plural. Antipode, one meaning of which is "the exact opposite," is pronounced—(AN-ti-pode). However its plural, antipodes, is pronounced—(an-TIP-i-deez).

Then there are all those silent letters that mess up our spelling! Once kids catch on, though, they love to pronounce these silent "Gs," just to sound silly:

Gnash
Gnarly
Gnat
Gnaw
Gnu

Or, what about something that's "flammable," which means it can ignite easily, and "INflammable," which of course means the same thing!

It's fun just to say some of our more unusual words out loud, like "lugubrious" (lu-GU-bree-us), which means overly mournful. Or, "obsequious" (ub-SEE-kwee-us), which means subservient.

Seeking out and having fun with strange spellings and oddly pronounced words can make a long car trip fly by, or take the "boring" out of a rainy summer day.

Be sure your children have dictionaries (starting with lots of pictures) from early on, and keep a favorite in an activity pack in the car. Give your children the right start by helping them learn to use the first and last word references at the tops of the pages and the simple pronunciation guides found throughout most dictionaries so they'll have the ability to look up and sound out words on their own. Vocabulary that they discover just "messing around" with their own dictionary is vocabulary that stays with them.

Having a rhyming dictionary on hand, too, can be beneficial and entertaining for the whole family. Children love asking others to come up with rhymes to a selected word. By looking for the words on the list and later reading the rest of the rhyming list aloud, they will be exposed both to the correct spelling of familiar words and to new words. Exposing them to a plethora (PLETH-ah-ra), a large number, of words early on gives them an interest in and fondness for words and wordplay.

Maybe your children have already surprised you with this pronunciation trick. If not, ask your seven-, eight-, or nine-year-old to pronounce what you spell. Deliver the letters as follows:

> BAS   (wait for pronunciation)
> EB   (wait for pronunciation)
> ALL   (wait for pronunciation)

Ask what word you get when you put it all together. It usually takes a few moments to get the word baseball! How could you break up other words in ways that lead someone to think it will be pronounced differently? Try MAC-HI-NE, SALAM-AND-ER, PA-PERB-ACK, DIE-SEL, IS-LAND. Now, make up your own.

Finally, the title of this chapter is GO GHOTI—What does it mean? It's an example of how letters take on different sounds within the context of words. In this case, we have constructed a "word" made up of letters from three different contexts. Each letter or combination of letters is not pronounced the way you'd expect it to sound. When you apply those pronunciations in this "word," you will decipher the puzzle. So now, to decode, read these words aloud slowly, emphasizing the capitalized letters as you say the words:

Ghoti (think GH + O + TI)
enouGH
wOmen
naTIon

Put those pronunciations together and what word do you get? Look for the answer at the end of the next chapter.[10]

Win-Win Word Game
Spelling and Vocabulary/Using the dictionary

RULES FOR 'DICTIONARY SARDINES' (for grade-schoolers)
Using a children's dictionary, the first player selects any *letter* of the alphabet as his *hideout*. For example, the letter "T." He copies down a word that begins with that letter and reads the definition aloud, before closing the dictionary. He first writes down "Tyrannosaurus Rex" then says aloud, "The largest and fiercest meat-eating dinosaur." Any player who thinks he knows what word is being defined takes the dictionary, opens to the same definition, and shows it to the player who selected the word without saying it aloud. If he has selected the correct word, he too is in the *hideout*.

The second player to the hideout then selects another word beginning with the same letter, for example, *thermometer*, writes it on the list, and reads that word's definition aloud: "An instrument for measuring temperature." If a third player recognizes either the first or the second word by definition, she, too, enters the hideout by showing the correct definition in the dictionary.

If a player is stumped, the players who are already in the hideout take turns selecting more words from the same hideout, adding each new word to the list and reading its definition aloud. Play continues until all players have been able to get into the hideout. The last player gets into the hideout, but does not choose a new word. Instead, she takes the list and reads all of the words aloud, waiting for each player to give a brief definition of his word. Play then goes to the first player to have correctly identified the hideout, who may now take the dictionary, pencil, and paper and select a word from a new hideout, that is, a different letter of the alphabet, for the next game.

'DICTIONARY SARDINES' is both a spelling and a vocabulary game. A familiar definition may belong to a word that is difficult to spell. If no one is able to find the first word, the first player gets to add another to the list himself. Using a *children's* dictionary is helpful both to limit the possibilities to familiar vocabulary, and because it offers pictures which can help less experienced spellers to find the definition. Be sure players get to take turns, checking as many possible spellings as they like. This game generates lists of words all beginning with the same letter, which can later be used to play alliteration games. Players should never say the words aloud—even in a whisper—until everyone makes it into the hideout.

CHAPTER TWENTY-TWO

Oxymorons

Today, there's hardly a town across America having more than two stoplights, that doesn't have an Asian restaurant. To our way of thinking that's praiseworthy of immigrants bringing their culture to a new country and forging a new life. And, more often than not, that restaurant features Chinese food—though Vietnamese, Thai, Korean, and Japanese cuisine are finding a ready clientele as well. On some of those menus you'll find sweet and sour pork, beef, shrimp, or vegetables—yumm! Sweet and sour is a tasty way of preparing food *and* a great introduction to oxymorons.

An oxymoron (OX-see-MOR-on) is a clever phrase which may at first glance seem incongruous or foolish. A *deafening silence* comes to mind. That might be a goofy thought to kids. "How can silence be deafening?" But we're sure a group of performers would find that oxymoron very apropos if, when they finished their performance, the audience sat quietly in their seats.

Have you known someone of whom you could say, "Deep down he is shallow"? Then there's that hard water or wicked good dessert to kick off a good mealtime conversation about oxymorons. Someone's deed may be perceived as cruel kindness, or attitude as haughty humility. (Two extra points for alliteration on those two!) And, we certainly don't want to pick even a friendly fight with any of our readers, but many people would include military intelligence as another good example.

As you can see, oxymorons can be subjective in nature—succinctly stated opinions. Point them out whenever you come across them as you read aloud, and encourage children to make up oxymorons to use in their own writing. You'll be giving them a tool to quickly emphasize a point or opinion—with the element of surprise. Here's an example:

> Mostly, the neighbors thought Tim was good. He would smile roundly with his hands behind his back, while bowing his head slightly and sliding a worn shoe through the dust. He'd tell them he was "right glad to see them," and that he'd "stop on by soon to fix the wagon and the latch that broke," and they'd think to themselves, "That Tim is a really good sort, he is." Only I knew Tim. I knew why he dropped his eyes, and shuffled nervously when neighbors walked by. But they never associated him with the rise in crime in town. Oh, he was good, all right. Terribly good—at lying.

That's obviously an example you'll want to teach your little ones *not* to emulate.

There are other ways in which you'll see your children living out oxymorons: when they're shyly precocious, devilishly angelic, or being sweetly obnoxious. Ah, the bitter-sweet joy of watching them grow into adulthood!

Write down you favorite oxymorons here as you play Jumbo Shrimp:

_____

_____

_____

_____

_____

_____

_____

Win-Win Word Game
Oxymorons

RULES FOR 'JUMBO SHRIMP' (for upper grade-schoolers)
To make up your own oxymorons,
   choose a characteristic,
   think of its opposite,
   turn the opposite into a descriptive word,
   and put them together in a sentence …

    ugly/exquisite … exquisitely ugly: The building was exquisitely
      ugly.
    good/terrible … terribly good: He was terribly good at lying.
    common/strange … strangely common: She was strangely
      common in appearance.

See how many oxymorons you can make up and write down in fifteen minutes. Choose your favorite or use one of ours to write a few sentences concluding with an oxymoron.

Read your paragraph aloud to each other. If someone doesn't know what oxymoron you are using, pause before revealing it. See if they come up with it before you say it aloud.

'JUMBO SHRIMP' is an opportunity for writing followed by reading aloud. Once written, this paragraph, like your child's other writings, can and should be shared aloud with family members, visitors—anyone who will accept the invitation (with your child's permission) to listen. Read original work aloud often. Make tape recordings to listen to in the car. Do all you can think of to promote and support the creative genius of your child.

Check it out!

10. Answer: enouGH   = F
                  wOmen   = I
                  naTIon   = SH
                  fish

CHAPTER TWENTY-THREE

Spoonerisms

Back in 1844 the man was born who would lend his name to a delightful and funny form of wordplay—spoonerisms.

The Reverend William Archibald Spooner was dean and warden of New College at Oxford from 1876 to 1924. But it was his verbal flusters when preaching that put the new word into the English language.

The hapless Rev. Spooner was never comfortable before a crowd, something we hope you and *Read it Aloud!* will help a shy child to overcome. When he became discombobulated (confused), Rev. Spooner would mix up his speech in a way that became popular enough in the English language to be named after him.

He might refer to the "queer old Dean" instead of the "dear old Queen." He preached about a "half-warmed fish" instead of a "half-formed wish." And then there's the line, jokingly attributed to him: "Mardon me padam, but this pie is occupewed; I will sew you to another sheet."

Once in the pulpit he said, "Our Lord is a shoving leopard." Oops! The good Reverend undoubtedly set off titters and guffaws in the congregation, and a well-turned spoonerism today can have kids howling with laughter. They'll also learn to listen carefully, and to think about the construction of words.

As a side note, spoonerisms can also be used to take the sting out of commands—and they sometimes help old words take on new urgency. For example, when your children come bouncing through the door and into the house with wet feet, don't shout, "Wipe your feet," try "Fipe your weet!" If you've got a group on your hands and you want them to get in line tell them to "let in gine," and remind them to "tait your wurn." They'll be happy to "jink their druice" at snack time. Spooner-isms can quite literally put a "file on the smaces" of your whole family!

Interestingly, *spoonerisms are a subset of a larger phenomenon called metathesis (muh-TATH-uh-sus), which is the transposition, or switching around, of sounds within a word or sentence.*

For example, some people will say "modren" instead of "modern," clapse instead of clasp, or brid instead of bird. Sometimes regionalisms in speech foster metathesis. We remember a character in Gunsmoke, an old western television series, saying: "You sure do look purtty (instead of pretty), Miss Kitty."

Now have some fun with your own spoonerisms—and watch for the giles and smiggles.

Note your family's "spavorite foonerisms" here:

Write them into a story here. Keep adding to the story as you
think of new spoonerisms.

_____

_____

_____

_____

_____

_____

_____

_____

_____

_____

_____

_____

_____

_____

_____

_____

_____

_____

_____

_____

Win-Win Word Game
Spoonerisms

RULES FOR 'PLEASE SASS THE PALT' (for all ages)
Wherever you are with your children, you can make up spoonerisms together. Any subject is fair game, but to help newcomers, have
a subject in mind. During a meal together you can practice with dinner communications, like: "Please sass the palt." When everyone
gets the idea, players can give a context by naming a location or
event: "You are at a rodeo …" Then everyone can have fun "translating" and making up their own spoonerism challenges about such
things as "bowboy coots" and "mild wustangs." You may choose to
focus only on objects you see in the room: "pellow yages," "trump
duck," and "bood gooks!" Write everyone's favorite creations down.
Someone may want to make up and record a story.

📖 📖 📖 📖

'PLEASE SASS THE PALT' may be easier for some players. Suggest
they help make up spoonerisms for others, perhaps even giving
everyone a spoonerism to figure out, so everybody has fun.

CHAPTER TWENTY-FOUR

Rhythm and Rhyme

Think how many songs, stories, and poems—words and feelings you remember from your childhood. At a glance you may remember the words to these:

> Twinkle … are.
> Roses … you.
> Row … dream.

Did you remember them as verses or songs? What elements of music and poetry make them so memorable?

In some cases it's rhyme. Each line leads you to expect something more—particularly couplets that end in a certain sound:

> The night settled down like the shell of a clam,
> And the pirates made ready to eat toast and …

You may never have heard these words together before, but you know it's "toast and jam."

The element of rhyme is satisfying to young children because it lets them predict the words before the message appears. Once heard, rhyme plays and replays in memory, enabling children to "read" rhyming passages long before they can decode words. As adults, we remember the nursery rhymes, counting out rhymes, acting out rhymes, skip-rope rhymes, and limericks of our childhood.

A tune behind the words makes the same kind of impression, whether there's a rhyme or not.

How many of us still hear the ditty of Walt Disney's Jiminy Cricket when we spell e-n-c-y-c-l-o-p-e-d-i-a? And what about advertising jingles—do those creep back into your thoughts at odd moments? It's no coincidence that *minstrels* carried official messages to public ears!

Rhythm, too, can firmly implant passages in our thought. Perhaps you can remember:

Half a league, half a league, half a league onward ...[11]
Whenever Richard Cory went downtown ...[12]
The wind was a torrent of darkness ...[13]

If you've ever memorized or heard any of these three powerful pieces read well, you not only remember some of the images and words, but the force, the cadence, and flow of it. And perhaps the voice which read it aloud to you.

The stories and poems you read aloud to your children today become memories of reading, laughing, and singing in the corridors of their minds tomorrow. Years later, favorite passages of stories and poems read aloud and songs sung will come back to enrich their lives.

What are you giving them to remember?

What have songwriters, storytellers, and poets given us to share? Through the years minstrels have given us their words and feelings just as they've felt them. When we sing their songs, and read their feelings, we breathe a living history. Plenty of poetry is being written today and we strongly recommend finding all kinds of works that you and your children can enjoy together. But take care not to miss out on the rich heritage of songs and poems that come from traditions, cultures, and times other than our own.[14]

As you select material to read aloud, you will find literature that is sometimes more, sometimes less well written for the ear. Look for stories on themes you wish to share, then check them out for rhythm, rhyme, imagery, and power. Your children will relate, respond to, and remember the messages of quality writing—and your voice, giving them the gift of literature.

Check it out!
11. *Charge of the Light Brigade*, by Alfred Tennyson
12. *Richard Cory*, by Edwin A. Robinson
13. *The Highwayman*, by Alfred Noyes
14. For first-hand insights into our nation's diverse cultural present and past, there's one book we thoroughly enjoy that contains over 140 traditional folktales and songs—with guitar chords and piano settings—reflecting the lives of Native Americans, slaves, and pioneers: *From Sea to Shining Sea, A Treasury of American Folklore and Folk Songs*, compiled by Amy L. Cohn (New York: Scholastic, Inc. 1993). The book is richly illustrated by Caldecott Award winners—those who have received awards for their artwork—and brings together themes for all ages and interests, including "scary, creepy, spooky ghost stories"; memorable baseball favorites, including Bud Abbott and Lou Costello's *Who's on First?*; historical essays; nonsense poems; and more.

You might also seek out *Celebrate America in Poetry and Art*, edited by Nora Panzer (New York: Hyperion Books for Children, 1994) (Ages 10 and up), featuring paintings, sculpture, drawings, photographs, and other works of art from the National Museum; *O Beautiful for Spacious Skies*, poems by Katharine Lee Bates with art by Wayne Thiebaud, edited by Sara Jane Boyers (San Francisco: Chronicle Books, 1994) (All ages); and the collection of songs selected by Wade and Cheryl Hudson with illustrations by Floyd Cooper, *How Sweet the Sound: African-American Songs for Children* (New York: Scholastic, Inc., 1995).

You've given me a relationship with my child.

Company president, engineer, Dad

PART THREE

COMMUNICATION, IMAGINATION, AND BOOKS!

The Reading Railroad

My two boys and I enjoy [stories] more through our increased interaction while reading.

Mechanical engineer, Dad

CHAPTER TWENTY-FIVE
Reading Gymnastics for Pre-K and K

E ven before your child is old enough to complain "There's nothing to do," you can establish a family tradition of turning to books, both for reading and as a source of shared activity. With young children, talking about characters and motives and plots while mixing in generous servings of imagination gives tremendous support to your children's ability to communicate.[15] Readiness to learn not only takes exposure to new concepts and ideas, but a supportive environment.[16]

With very young children, you'll often be asked to read the same story over and over again—sometimes just after you've finished reading it. While you may not always be able to deliver, realize it's more than seconds on dessert they're asking for. There are many benefits attached to rereading books.

Each time you reread a story to very young children, they have the pleasure of knowing what's coming up next and anticipating the good parts: The fun voices. The surprise part. The scary part. The resolution. As adult readers, we will often reread choice passages of a novel for the same reasons. In addition, your very young children are mastering new skills. In rereading to them they get more out of the pictures. They learn more of the story. They learn to turn pages, understand the relationship of type to the pictures, and how to read from left to right and top to bottom. In fact, it's helpful to use your hand to trace the words you're reading. Then one day you'll see them imitating your reading. They'll be reading books themselves, from the repetition and memory and associations they've formed. The mastery of the content of a book takes time on their part—and yes, a lot of patience on yours!

While there are also numerous ways to share *new* ideas as you reread those *familiar* books, don't hesitate to introduce new books. If you can, give your children a choice that includes an old favorite and their preference in something new. Going to the library and getting that first library card can add to the excitement of reading new books.

Now let's look at some specific suggestions for sharing books—old or new—starting at the infant/toddler stages. Learning to share books interactively, rather than having children listen passively, is especially helpful to your preschooler. Once you see how it works, you'll be coming up with many fun and creative ideas of your own. In some cases we've noted developmental benefits or skills associated with an activity, but keep in mind that any reading aloud—and simultaneous or follow-up book-related discussion and activity that you share—can contribute to your child's self-confidence, intellectual development, social skills, and ease of communication.

These are just a few ideas to get you started:

1. Interactive reading can be touch—push—pull—taste!

Even before little ones find their toes, they are ready to grab and chew books. That's OK—quality board books, made of heavy cardboard and nontoxic inks, are designed for the very young. These early books for children involve them in a variety of activities and responses, enabling you to help your child focus her attention for increasingly longer periods of time as she grows. Designed to be interactive, many of these books involve the infant/toddler in doing something on every page.

Many of us grew up with a board book called *Pat the Bunny* by Dorothy Kunhardt.[17] You turn each cardboard page and help your child "feel Daddy's scratchy face," which is a piece of sandpaper, "look in the mirror," or whatever it tells you to do. Page-turning itself is an introduction to books and book activity. As you get excited and smile and play, you convey the pleasure and fun of books, which your baby loves sharing with you.

Right from the start, you can begin to connect what you read to your child with the activity in her life. The next time you see Daddy's scratchy beard on Daddy, encourage your baby to "feel Daddy's scratchy face." Find a mirror in the house and "look in the mirror!" Use the language of the book as you enjoy the experience, and the correlation of the book to real life becomes clearer. Before going to a real petting zoo, read *The Petting Zoo* by Jack Hanna,[18] where your baby touches imitation fur and feathers and velvety horns and hard tusks.

Wheels Go Round by Yvonne Hooker,[19] with illustrations by Carlo A. Michelini, is another type of interactive book with holes that little fingers can poke through. Other books have buttons or figures to push, tabs to pull, or panels to lift. As your toddler wins your praise and encouragement by reaching out and touching or turning the page, you are building confidence, as well as a love for books.

2. Interactive reading can be noisy!

As you read aloud to infants and toddlers, look for books that have rhythm and rhyme! Why? Learning to speak a language involves patterns of sounds as well as words. You want to share the joy and poetry of language whenever you can. Alternately clap your baby's hands and your own to the rhythms of the rhymes you're sharing.

With toddlers you'll find that as they get more familiar with a rhyme, they can help you "read." They may or may not be able to actually read the words—but they know them. So play a little. Hesitate on key words: "... the mouse ran up the ..." and your children will chime in "clock!" That's reading together. And it's fun.

Sound effects are a fun part of reading aloud, too. You might try having your children participate by doing sound effects with you when called for. But remember, kids love it when you surprise them with sounds and voices, so ask yourself what sounds the words or pictures conjure up, and bring them to life!

One subject that seems to fascinate young children is construction. If there's interest on your child's part, look for books about front loaders and dump trucks. When there's activity in your neighborhood, pack a book with a picnic and head for the site. Talk about everything you see going on, looking in the book to identify and learn more about the vehicles you're watching. Have fun with the Richard Scarry[20] books, which are chock full of tiny hardworking characters using hand tools and driving front loaders. You could relate pictures to your personal experiences together, like: "I'm looking at something we saw move dirt at the construction site yesterday," or, "We need to go to the store to get some fruit. What kind of fruit car should we drive to the store today?"

3.   Interactive reading can be observation games!

Give directional hints about where an object is on the page, and in relation to other figures. Children who start preschool knowing the terms top, bottom, under, over, left, right, center are more likely to feel comfortable receiving instructions. Introduce these words and more, in this and other contexts. It's also useful to introduce comparisons. You can easily compare the size and color of one object to other figures: "I'm looking at something that's bigger than the bird, and the same color as the tree."

Even while you and your child are sharing these simple observations you can begin the lifelong process of using literature to promote your child's decision-making and problem-solving skills:

Learning to make choices can begin with wordless books, as in *Let's Look at Animals* by Dick Witt.[21] You can ask questions that children control the answers to by applying their imagination and values: "Is the monkey going to eat all the bananas or save some for later? Does he have any to share?" Be sure to keep it fun by mixing this kind of dialogue with imitating sounds, pretending to feed the animals, finding the bird that's sitting and the ones that are flying, etc. When you consider the possibilities for relating the pictures in picture books to real life, you'll find that discussion topics are truly unlimited.

Wordless books also have their place in reading aloud with older children. Without the limitations of concrete wording, readers can convey their own feelings and strong messages. For example, one powerful, out-of-print European wordless book called *The Expedition*[22] leads the "reader" to understand the emotions and betrayal felt when one culture invades and plunders another. The friend who introduced this book to us said it was a favorite in her family and noted that with each telling, the story evolved, becoming richer through the years. Everyone in the family was able to communicate personal bits of wisdom, while developing the plot.

4. Interactive reading can be manipulating words and ideas to create humor!

In his book *Hey! Listen to This*[23] Jim Trelease describes the interactive Little *Green* Riding Hood, a quirky style of storytelling inspired by every parent's eventual exasperation with retelling the same story. Far from being unpleasant, the misstatement of the familiar version of a story has a certain appeal because the child enjoys making the corrections.

This same concept can be applied to concept and object identification in picture books. For example, while color identification is still a new enough skill that "getting it right" builds self-esteem, but you're sure your child is perfectly clear on which color is which, you can look at bunny's red shoes and say, "Look at that bunny's blue shoes! Aren't they pretty?" Even though your child realizes you're kidding, she'll enjoy telling you the shoes are not blue, they're red. To let her know that she is right, and to build her self-esteem, don't forget to confirm and offer praise for what she has learned: "Oh yes! Red shoes! You're right!"

Another time, you might casually comment on the pictures of familiar animals, mentioning the lion's bold black and white stripes, and the long trunk on the monkey. You'll be rewarded with a happy chorus of giggles and protests.

Here's a discussion game that delights children, and lets them be funny right with you. You can see the wheels of analytical thinking turning as the sparkle in their eyes is turned into ideas of their own. When they "get it" and respond, they've embraced a new, humorous line of communication—a joke that can be told again and again about different subjects. Start with a question or two based on the book as you're looking at a picture, then broaden it to your child's life experience:

"What if the door were too big for the house?"

"What if you got up one morning and the sun were too big for the sky?" Or in the area of getting dressed:

"What if you got mixed up and put your shoes on before your socks!"

"What if you got mixed up and put your gloves on your elbows?"

They love to laugh over these ideas, and quickly volunteer their own parallel ideas.

You might also try nonsense using opposites. If you're walking along on a beautiful day you might suggest:

"The sun is too cold and wet. Let's dry off in the shade."

We almost guarantee a positive reaction. And it can lead to discussion, and to books. You might like to talk about weather and what it makes us do—how we have to dress in special ways for weather, for example. Then go to the bookshelf and pull out a story about weather.[24]

5. Interactive reading can be discussing detailed drawings!

Some illustrations are in and of themselves a type of problem-solving activity. While building a child's attention span, examining the intricacies of minutely detailed illustrations is not unlike decoding printed words, especially distinguishing the subtle differences among the four most confusing lower case letters (b, d, p, q). The series of *Where's Waldo?*[25] books challenge young readers to pick out something that's different (Waldo himself), which is done with humor and design. Who finds Waldo first in your family? If it's not one of the children, we hope you let them think it is! When you read them together, books with detailed drawings can improve communication skills. For example, listening:

Let's say a child knows where Waldo is and you (supposedly) don't. Using verbal directions only, that is, without pointing, see if you can describe to her a part of the picture that *you* are looking at. Have her find your figure and put her finger on it. Then you pick another figure nearby and describe it until she finds it. Ask her if you are getting warmer or cooler in relation to Waldo. You can gauge her interest level and decide whether or not to take some major tangents getting to Waldo. An exaggerated miss or two can, of course, add to the excitement.

Listening *and* verbal skills are developed when you *take turns* giving hints about an object in an illustration until the other can figure out what it is. A beautiful book we recommend is *Abuela*, by Arthur Dorros,[26] with vibrant illustrations by Elisa Kleven. This story of a young girl and her grandmother's visit to the park becomes an adventure of flying with the birds. The cheerful, colorful, highly detailed illustrations lend themselves to close study, discussion, and imagining together.

You'll also want to seek and find with the *I Spy* series of art books, devised and selected by Lucy Micklethwait. Each book has its own "flavor." One might feature a profusion of objects from M&M's to beads, another intricate pictures modeled in clay. In *I Spy a Freight Train: Transportation in Art*[27] you'll find photographs of different styles and periods of art from around the world. Your very young children will be asked to look for a rowboat in one picture, a hot air balloon, wagon, or camel in others. Older children, too, can appreciate and interact with the art.

To enjoy exquisitely rich illustrations, while stretching every family member's vocabulary, share *Animalia*, by Graeme Base.[28] Pleasing to the eye, this marvelous excursion to twenty-six alphabet letter-based locations can be explored by several children of different ages at one time. The paintings are designed to be pored over for hours, challenging readers to use enough imagination to find and identify hundreds of objects.

You'll also want your entire family to enjoy the clever creations of Joan Steiner in *Look-Alikes*,[29] where you'll find recognizable city scenes entirely made up of household objects. It's a marvel—and it comes with its own activity guide.

6. Interactive reading can be exploring a new way of seeing together!

Let your child know there is a person called an illustrator who made the pictures. You can suppose reasons the illustrator made certain choices. For example, one of our favorites is *Owl Moon* by Jane Yolen, with illustrations by John Schoenherr.[30] You can talk about perspective: Point out that you're seeing the house and barn from way up in the trees and ask, "Why do you think the illustrator of *Owl Moon* drew the house so far down below like that?" Or you can put your child into the illustrator's place: "What objects, animals, or people would *you* put on the page?" "How could you make these pictures look more like summer?"

Abuela, or its sequel, *Isla*, is also a fine selection for discussing perspective. You might ask your child what she thinks the bird's-eye view of your own residence, school, library, or any unusual town buildings might look like. If she has appropriate materials available, she might, on her own, decide to draw it one day.

7. Interactive reading can be discussion at snack time!

With four and five year olds it sometimes is helpful to have a focus at snack time or mealtime. With hints of your own you might start a guessing game about a book's theme or character. Be ready to take turns, starting with the child that guessed the first answer. For example: "I am thinking of a character who tricks everyone into helping him." Give more hints until a child comes up with the answer. You might have several books handy for when the game ends.

8. Interactive reading can be story-based snack preparation!

If you suspect Winnie-the-Pooh has been helping himself to your honey, think of all the recipes he might use them for. Have your children plan and prepare lunch, using honey recipes. The next time you read a book that mentions food, you'll have eager bakers-in-waiting. While you might need time to arrange your schedule, be sure to follow up within a few days, to keep the book/activity association fresh. You might even kick off the event by rereading the appropriate part of the story, or by looking closely at the picture to compare your kitchen and tools with those used in the story.

9. Interactive reading can be inviting a storybook friend to lunch!

Try thinking of the characters you meet as mutual friends. Those friends make decisions that you would like to discuss, and have your child remember. So do something memorable …

You might set the scene for a discussion by inviting a character, say Peter Rabbit, to your home—once you know what he likes to eat, of course. You might ask how to let Peter know he's invited. Your child might call out the window, or design and post an invitation. Let the writing of an invitation be her idea, not an assignment. Then plan, shop for, and make a special salad together. Set Peter's place at the table, hear the knock at the door (rap on the table), invite him in, and talk with him during lunch. "Oh, you do like peas? I'm so glad we put some in your salad. And carrots, because they are so long and orange and sweet? Oh, and you've never had them sliced before? We forgot, didn't we, 'cause we almost always slice them for ourselves. What can we do? He'd rather have it whole!" Your child may suggest going to the refrigerator to get another, or she may just giggle. Follow through if you can, or suggest that next time you'll fix one just the way he wants it. In any case, you are giving your child the opportunity to analyze the situation and use *her* imagination.

Take the lead on digging into the options Peter had when he chose to go into Farmer McGreggor's garden. Ask Peter if he had other choices, and after waiting for a response, ask your child if she could suggest any. Point out the consequences of his decision and let your child come up with what would have happened if a different choice had been made.

By talking about Peter's choices, you are encouraging your child to think more when it comes to a decision she faces. If your child later says, "Look who's sitting at the table, Dad," you know the visit was a success, and she's ready for more. Keep that communication channel open! Someday it may be a boyfriend sitting there, and your memorable discussions with imaginary characters will help your daughter to think about—and discuss—her boyfriend's character, motives, and actions—and her own choices.

10. Interactive reading can be role-play!

If you plan to suggest acting out a story or scene, children will benefit from discussing the feelings of the characters beforehand, just after you read the story together. If you have a group, you may wish to specify that you will act something out twice, so everyone gets to try two roles.

Are you familiar with the story *Caps for Sale*, told and illustrated by Esphyr Slobodkina?[31] Try reading this book to several children, then later, when you're on the playground, ask who wants to be a peddler (more than one is fine; if none, you can be the peddler), and who wants to be a monkey. The monkeys climb into the monkey bars, and the peddlers put on their caps and walk around until they need a rest by the monkey bars. The monkeys all sneak down and take caps off the peddlers' heads and scamper back up. Then the peddlers wake up and shout at the monkeys, shaking their fists. The monkeys will have a great time imitating the peddlers and shouting, "Chi! Chi! Chi!" back at them. Then the peddlers get angrier and stamp their feet and the monkeys do the same. Then the peddlers throw their last caps down on the ground in frustration, and the little monkeys do the same. The peddlers gather the caps up, stack them up on their heads and begin to hawk their caps again, calling "Caps for Sale!"

It's a great story to read before you go to the park. And it's memorable enough that you can recharge your children's interest in books by bringing it up for a smile in the middle of winter:

As you're flipping through scarves and gloves looking for hats, let your children hear you think aloud, "I wonder if those monkeys from *Caps for Sale* came into our closet? I'm having trouble finding all our caps!"

You might conclude that the monkeys have eaten at your table while you were outside, perhaps by finding an imaginary banana peel. If you have a dramatic streak in you, you might even go further. Set up an ambush and have your very young children help you place imaginary bananas in strategic places overnight. Do you think your kids will remember to check to see if the monkeys came? You can count on it!

11. Interactive reading can be acting out poems!

I have spent many happy hours with Shel Silverstein's poetry,[32] children, and a staging area. We worked on the basics of oral presentation: learning to project the voice, posture that gives strength, and breathing from the diaphragm. Kids choreographed, acted, and directed with a level of excitement we often associate with sports.

One site was an afterschool. The grades ranged from K–6, and attendance was voluntary. Assisted by my friend Pat O'Brien, I began each session with a favorite group warm-up: reciting tongue-twisters. When we broke up, kids chose from the sheets of poems we'd duplicated, forming smaller performance groups—solo, partners, or teams—who then began rehearsing. We coached and gave nonreaders help learning their poems, but let them make their own decisions about how to act them out. Whenever a poem was "ready," we'd break and gather in front of a makeshift stage to watch the performers. We also selected an assistant director from among the children and one poem for the entire group to perform together. This culminated, by popular demand, in a rewarding collective performance for other children attending the afterschool.

12. Interactive reading can be a book-theme costume party!

This idea applies to your teddy bear set—everyone comes as and with their favorite bear—or to your growing grade-schooler. Choose any favorite group of characters, and invite friends. Consider an *American Girls Collection*[33] tea party. Children who are reading the series and collecting the dolls have great models for dressing up. At tea-time, have a parent familiar with the stories lead a discussion about how each girl feels about the events she's experiencing. Look for local clubs or bookstores that are already sponsoring teas in your area.

13. Interactive reading can be putting ideas down on paper!

If you have created "Writing Boxes" for each child (an appropriate assortment of writing tools and surfaces specifically selected to match your children's abilities and interests, whether preschoolers or grade-schoolers), and understand the "rules" that go with them ("Bill of Writes"), you just might find your children coming to you with illustrations that show different perspectives or seasons—of the books you've discussed or another they've begun. From there you have new stories to discuss, and opportunities to build a library of books by your children.

The "Writing Boxes" and "rules" we're referring to are explained in a book we feel no parent or teacher should be without that develops this subject of helping children put their ideas down on paper: *Kids Have All The Write Stuff*, by Sharon A. Edwards and Robert W. Maloy.[34] The subtitle, *Inspiring Your Children to Put Pencil (or crayon or felt-tip marker or computer) to Paper*, hints at the fact that all children, even the very young who cannot yet write all of the alphabet letters, love writing when they know it means choosing when and how to put their own ideas down on paper. The book keeps you from falling into the traps that make creative writing a chore for children. It also shows you ways to introduce "book spelling," or the correct spelling of words, for publication. In addition, they've thoughtfully indexed fun books that inspire creative writing— for preschoolers on up. They've even explained how to talk with children about their writing, and provided a variety of ways to bind home-made books.

To encourage original work by your kids, first write something *together*, which can inspire children to try again later on their own. As you know, you can't *force* anyone to love something. But if you *share* something, you impart its value as well.

Here are a few suggestions:

PEN AND PAD

- Read other versions of the same story, illustrated by different artists, then write and illustrate a version of your own.
- Make a rebus (island = drawing of an eye + land) of the story.
- Design a crossword puzzle using everything in one of the story's pictures.
- Re-illustrate, picking a new season for the story. Include designing appropriate seasonal clothing for characters.
- Illustrate the story from a different spatial perspective.
- Make a flipbook with facial expressions showing the changing feelings of a character throughout the story.
- Recreate the story with puppets, scenery, and props. Do your own shows, including programs and invitations.
- Design hats to wear when you act out different roles from the story.
- Make mobiles of the story elements: characters, furniture or objects, buildings or trees, and the names of the book, the author, and the illustrator.

- Do pictures that combine drawings and paste-ups with rubbings of mobile story elements. To do the rubbings, place cutouts under a sheet of paper, then rub the paper with the side of a crayon until the shapes appear. It might be fun to draw faces onto the rubbings of bears, for example, combined with rubbings or drawings of tables, chairs, and beds, adding pasted colored-paper cutouts of bedspreads and porridge bowls for Goldilocks and the Three Bears.
- Make mazes featuring heroes and villains from the story.
- Draw chalk footprints of the story's characters on the sidewalk.
- Try a line/hole/shape/footprint/sticker or stamp story: Pre-mark each sheet of paper with any one of the above, then develop the art and story around the mark.
- Shoot a photo story: Take pictures then tell a story to go with them.
- Create an artwork story: Tell what happened—as a painter.

Of course you can use your *computer* to be creative after reading aloud, too. Have your children use spell check to begin making corrections, but be sure to point out the need to ignore many computer-generated grammar suggestions, and to proof all writing for the types of spelling errors the computer won't catch. As an example, have your children type: "Eyed bee care full!" to see what computerized spelling and grammar assistance is offered. Of course, in spite of their limitations, computers are tools your children will need to become very comfortable with. So, what can you do on a computer together? After reading a story, you can blend your imaginations, talk through different ideas, then write and edit as a team. You might even have your child type left hand keys while you type right hand keys, to help get a feel for where letters are on a keyboard. As soon as possible, find software that teaches them to use all of their fingers on the keyboard. More specifically, you can share more about writing and computers if you …

ON THE COMPUTER

- Write a song or poem about the story, copying and pasting refrains.
- Write acrostics. (Write each letter of a character's name or selected word on a separate line; use each letter to start a new sentence.) Make a point of learning to set and use tabs.
- Make up tongue twisters and rhymes about the story characters.
- Rewrite the story from a different character's perspective. Try using two columns to split the story in two.
- Change the story's cast to make it about your own family. Retell the story in script form using original character names, then search, find, and replace with names of family and friends. Print different versions of your script.
- Add a page, chapter, or new ending to the book. Match the page format and font, print, cut to size, and keep it with the original story for repeated enjoyment when reading the story aloud. Or you can copy portions of what you've written into different documents, submitting them for different endings by siblings. Be sure to include a line for the author's identity.
- You might even want to write your own stories from scratch—or from one of these springboards:

> Chris Van Allsburg has put together a book of eerie drawings with captions as story-starters called *The Mysteries of Harris Burdick*,[35] which we highly recommend for grade-schoolers.

> "All about" books can be written on any subject you choose: Me, rocks, butterflies, or a geographical area of interest. Try a location as small as "All about the inside of my closet" or "… refrigerator."

> Personal experience story: Have very young children dictate a story from play. Write plot as developed while playing, or, if

your child was unhappy, write the story the way he thinks it would have been better.

SFX story: Write and record to audio tape a story using plenty of sound effects (SFX). Sony makes a large, plastic tape recorder, suitable for home or school use by younger children.

Your favorite books, reread in the light of any of these suggestions, will bring many more fresh ideas and activities to mind. Your children's inspirations, too, will keep books at the center of family activity where they belong. As your children grow and change, so will their choice of book-based activities.

What won't change, however, is the benefit of an increased level of communication as growing and changing interests are shared and enjoyed.

Check it out!

15. "Reading a book to a child shouldn't just be a rote exercise. It's not just reading the words, but having interesting conversations about the book that helps children build stronger oral-language skills." Patton Tabors, research coordinator of the Home-School Study. *Harvard Education Letter* 1997, Vol. 13, No. 4 page 2.

16. "Early literacy development is supported by experiences of many types that occur in varied settings. Its roots draw nourishment from oral language experiences that occur in the home, from activities in classrooms that include use of books or otherwise support rich language use, and from experiences with print in all settings. Parents and teachers eager to foster growth of early literacy skills need to be encouraged to challenge children's minds and discursive language abilities in addition to providing functional and varied experiences with print." *Journal of Research in Childhood Education* 1991, Vol. 6. No. 1 page 30. David K. Dickinson, Clark University and Patton O. Tabors, Harvard

Graduate School of Education. Copyright 1991 by the Association for Childhood Education International 0256-8543/91

17. Dorothy Kunhardt, *Pat the Bunny* (New York: Western Publishing Company, Inc., 1942).

18. Jack Hanna, *The Petting Zoo* (New York: Doubleday, 1992).

19. English translation by Yvonne Hooker, *Wheels Go Round*, (New York: Grosset & Dunlap, 1990).

20. *Richard Scarry's Cars and Trucks and Things that Go* (New York: A Golden Book, 1974).

21. Dick Witt, *Let's Look at Animals* (New York: Scholastic, 1993).

22. Willi Baum, *The Expedition* (Glasgow and London: Blackie, 1976).

23. Jim Trelease, *Hey! Listen to This: Stories to Read Aloud* (New York: Penguin Books, 1992), p.8. If you don't have this or any of Jim's other essential resources in your family collection, go get *The Read-Aloud Handbook* today (also Penguin, 1995). Now in its fourth edition, this book gives practical help to all parents, including those who would like to reintroduce reading aloud into a busy family that isn't used to sitting down to listen to a book. It also contains a "giant treasury" of read-aloud books. For more information about reading aloud, and a preview of resources Jim has developed, see his website: <www.trelease-on-reading.com> And we encourage anyone—especially new dads—to take in his extraordinarily entertaining and helpful lecture.

24. Board Books: Satoshi Kitamara, *Duck is Dirty* (New York: Farrar, Straus, & Giroux, 1996), first published in Great Britain by Andersen Press, 1996); or, learn to count from one to twenty as you enjoy "beautiful color illustrations and strong images of children learning, sharing and playing together" on a wet and rainy day as illustrated by Jan Spivey Gilchrist with "delicate, funny and loving language" by Eloise Greenfield, *Aaron and Gayla's Counting Book* (New York: Black Butterfly Children's Books by Writers and Readers Publishing Inc., 1993).

Picture books: Ezra Jack Keats, *The Snowy Day* (New York: Puffin Books, 1962) or by Marie Hall Ets, *Gilberto and the Wind* (also Puffin, 1978). There's also an Æsop's tale about kindness, called *The Sun and the Wind*.

25. Martin Handford, *Where's Waldo?* (Cambridge: Candlewick Press, 1997).

26. Arthur Dorros, *Abuela* (New York: Dutton Children's Books, 1991); also *Isla*, 1995.

27. Lucy Micklethwait, *I Spy a Freight Train: Transportation in Art* (New York: Greenwillow Books, 1996).

28. Graeme Base, *Animalia* (New York: Harry N. Abrams, Inc., 1986).

29. Joan Steiner, *Look Alikes* (Boston: Little, Brown & Company, 1998).

30. Jane Yolen, *Owl Moon* (New York: Philomel Books, 1987).

31. Esphyr Slobodkina, *Caps for Sale: A tale of a peddler, some monkeys, and their monkey business* (New York: HarperCollins, 1984).

32. Shel Silverstein's poetry and drawings: *Where the Sidewalk Ends* (New York: HarperCollins, 1974), *A Light in the Attic* (New York: HarperCollins, 1981), and *Falling Up* (New York: HarperCollins, 1996). Also look for his stories: *The Giving Tree* (New York: Harper & Row, 1964), and *The Missing Piece Meets the Big O* (New York: HarperCollins, 1981).

33. *American Girls Collection* (Middleton, WI: Pleasant Co.). Over twenty books by several authors.

34. Sharon A. Edwards and Robert W. Maloy, *Kids Have All the Write Stuff, Inspiring Your Children to Put Pencil (or crayon or felt-tip marker or computer) to Paper* (New York: Penguin Books, Inc., 1992). Sharon won a 1990 Good Neighbor Award from State Farm Insurance Companies and the National Council of Teachers of English for starting the Writing Box project with her students.

35. Chris Van Allsburg, *The Mysteries of Harris Burdick* (Boston: Houghton Mifflin Company, 1984).

CHAPTER TWENTY-SIX

Fostering Grade-School Readers

Our imaginations put us in touch with our feelings, sometimes before we even can put ideas into words.

Consider a poem by Lewis Carroll, author of *Alice in Wonderland*, called *Jabberwocky:*

'Twas brillig, and the slithy toves
Did gyre and gimble in the wabe:
All mimsy were the borogoves,
And the mome raths, outgrabe.

"Beware the Jabberwock, my son!
The jaws that bite, the claws that catch!
Beware the Jubjub bird, and shun
The frumious Bandersnatch!"

He took his vorpal sword in hand:
Long time the manxome foe he sought—
So rested he by the Tumtum tree,
And stood awhile in thought.

And, as in uffish thought he stood,
The Jabberwock, with eyes of flame,
Came whiffling through the tulgey wood,
And burbled as it came!

One, two! One two! And through and through
The vorpal blade went snicker-snack!
He left it dead, and with its head,
He went galumphing back.

"And hast thou slain the Jabberwock?
Come to my arms, my beamish boy!
"Oh frabjous day! Callooh, Callay!"
He chortled in his joy!

'Twas brillig, and the slithy toves
Did gyre and gimble in the wabe:
All mimsy were the borogoves,
And the mome raths outgrabe.

What was the setting? What's the point?

According to Francelia Butler in her commentary/anthology *Sharing Literature with Children*:

> This brilliant nonsense poem, which has been analyzed by linguists, logicians, and philosophers, as well as literary critics, made its first appearance in 1855 (first stanza only) as a parody of Anglo-Saxon poetry, and reappeared in *Through the Looking Glass* (1871) as a longer poem. Alice describes it as well as anyone: "It seems very pretty," she said when she had finished it, "but it's rather hard to understand! ... Somehow it seems to fill my head with ideas—only I don't exactly know what they are! However, somebody *killed* something: *that's clear, at any rate—*"[36]

One of the rewards of reading aloud is that you and your children can share the *feelings* a poem or story introduces. You can read it over and over just for the sounds and dramatic tension. You can memorize the whole thing or just bits and snatches. You can talk about its imaginary setting, characters, and action. You can stop and talk, laugh, or cry together. Discussing stories about *imaginary* characters and situations can build *very real* communication between you and your children.

When your children take interest in a plot, it means they can project their own feelings into a situation. At least for the moment they are able to identify with one or more of a character's traits or circumstances. That's when the story becomes a microcosm of life to *them*, and your children are actively choosing heroes and heroines as they analyze, and take in, a story's message. Sharing books by reading aloud puts you at the threshold of your children's feelings and ideas, which far exceed their reading abilities. Being sensitive to literature's emotional content, you can bring children the issues and drama in books three to four grade levels beyond their own reading level up until they're in high school. But what should you read?

This is where the library, more than a repository for books, affords you invaluable aid as a read-aloud parent.

Librarians try to stay abreast of newly published books that address contemporary issues. They have resources that catalogue books by subject[37] and are only too happy to help you find the right books for you to read aloud with your family. Even smaller libraries will be able to direct you to the Newbery Medal winners, the Caldecott Award winners, the Coretta Scott King Award winners, the Horn Book Award winners, and the American Booksellers Association pick of the list. But you must be selective when you're supplementing your children's own reading diet. Don't just pick books off a "health food" list without looking into the content.

To win and hold their attention, apply what you've learned from them! Look for book reviews that focus on your children's interests.[38] It may be as broad a classification as, say, adventure. Or after you've talked about their personal challenges, go to the library or bookstore to look for books with characters who face or address those issues. So long as stories are relevant to their interests or lives, children will listen—and benefit.

Preread and pick something that addresses your child's growing understanding. E.B. White's Charlotte teaches us for example, not to give up hope and to think our way out of difficulties as she kindly uses her cleverness to save an innocent victim in *Charlotte's Web*.[39] Others use their cleverness for self-preservation.[40]

If you're trying to communicate with a child about sensitive issues your family and children are dealing with, ask a librarian to guide you to books designed to open discussion about those topics.[41] This is often referred to as bibliotherapy.

To initiate or rekindle a love of reading, you should also be aware that there are scores of magazines specializing in the interests of children of all ages. A subscription sent to them at home often can build a positive association with reading, even spark an eager anticipation of reading, in any young person. If your children are not already subscribing to the magazines focused on their special interests, take a field trip to the bookstore or library to see what interests them. If your library is unable to show you copies of magazines but has a list, get the toll-free numbers and give them a call. We've listed a few magazines that you should be aware of for infants and toddlers on up. (See Appendix II.) Often, publishers will send you a free sample. If you possibly can, when you find a magazine that catches your child's interest, get a subscription. In the long run it's a small price to pay for the incentive to read.

One parent was commenting that she had been concerned that her son was reading about drug users in a popular teen magazine. His reading, however, didn't kindle an interest in drugs. To her everlasting delight and surprise, he became fascinated with life stories, and went on to read many full-fledged biographies of performers and musicians.

Spend a few minutes at the library learning—and teaching your children eight and over—how to use the *Children's Magazine Guide*.[42] This will add excitement and a level of fulfillment to any reading your child wishes to do on personal favorite subjects, and is a positive and practical way to introduce periodical research skills.

Choosing to read a book rather than to plop down in front of a TV sitcom or to challenge a computer game takes a certain expectation on your child's part—one of enjoyment and fulfillment. Book series can nurture that eager expectation. For many grade-schoolers, the ever-expanding Redwall series[43] has introduced courageous role models who prefer nonviolence. Older children can identify and be strengthened by Brian's courage in the series of survival books by Gary Paulson.[44] The Narnia series[45] is a long-standing classic, and the more recently introduced—and probably instant classic—Harry Potter series[46] is so original in its "special effects" that it has turned reluctant readers into avid readers in the blink of an eye. You can be part of these adventures, reading aloud to inspire your grade-schoolers to rediscover the pleasures of reading. You can help them make the connection between literature and their own needs and interests.

When do you stop? Well, when do you want to stop thinking, dreaming, solving problems, and discussing issues together? You don't have to stop at all. You can make a permanent place for the fun of reading aloud and sharing —*imagination*! Learning together, wondering what will happen together, imagining together, laughing and thinking together as you explore literature that meets your children's sensibilities, gives you much to communicate about—and establishes the quest to understand life—through books.

Check it out!

36. Francelia Butler, *Sharing Literature with Children* (New York: Longman, Inc. 1977). This unparalleled rich compendium of intriguing children's literature will supply you with fresh views and practical tools for engaging your children in reading for a lifetime. Also look up books by Lucy Calkins, *Raising Lifelong Learners, A Parent's Guide* (Reading, MA: Addison-Wesley, 1997) and Bernice Cullinan, *Read to Me: Raising Kids Who Love to Read* (New York: Scholastic, 1992).

37. Ask for the latest update of this book: Eden Ross Lipson, *The New York Times Parent's Guide to the Best Books for Children* (New York:

Times Books, 1988). You may want to keep a copy on your home bookshelf.

38. We encourage you to read selections from the read-aloud sampling anthology by Jim Trelease, *Hey! Listen to This: Stories to Read Aloud* (New York: Penguin Books, 1992) to see what might interest your child. Jim includes fascinating insights into the lives of the authors, and lists his choice of other outstanding anthologies. We also recommend independent children's bookstores, whose owners specialize in connecting children to the right books.

    To match books to children's interests we also highly recommend two resource books by Kathleen Odean, *Great Books for Girls* (Ballantine, 1997) and *Great Books for Boys* (Ballantine, 1998). Both are conveniently designed to guide parents through age and type classifications of selections —Picture-Story Books, Folktales, Books for Beginning Readers, Books for Middle Readers, and Books for Older Readers. These are further divided into subsections that pinpoint interests and needs. Fiction includes Adventure and Survival, Historical Fiction, Contemporary Novels, Humorous Stories, Sports Fiction, Mysteries and Ghost Stories, Fantasy and Science Fiction. Biographies include subsections of Leaders and Activists; Artists, Musicians, and Writers; Scientists and Inventors; etc. The Nonfiction classification introduced in her second book, *Great Books for Boys*, features History, Nature and Science, Technology, Hobbies and Sports, and Poetry. Each description thoughtfully characterizes the feel of a book, summarizes its story line, and provides publishing information.

39. E.B. White *Charlotte's Web* (New York: HarperCollins, 1952).

40. Don't miss Newbery Medalist Virginia Hamilton's *A Ring of Tricksters: Animal tales from America, the West Indies, and Africa* (New York: Scholastic, 1997). Written in native storytelling styles,

each tale is accompanied by National Book Award-winner Barry Moser's spirited and unforgettable art.

41. In Dr. Thomas Lickona's latest excellent book, *Raising Good Children* (New York: Bantam Books, 1994), the 120 books he and his wife list for reading and discussing include recommendations from: *The Heartwood Ethics Curriculum for Children* (a literature-based program they recommend to schools wishing to teach good values: Heartwood Institute, 12300 Perry Highway, Wexford, PA 15090. 412-934-1777); Elizabeth Baird Saenger's *Exploring Ethics Through Children's Literature* (another of their recommended school resources available from Critical Thinking Press and Software, P.O. Box 448, Pacific Grove, CA 93950-0448); and a third source, whose recommendation we heartily echo, is William Kilpatrick's book, *Why Johnny Can't Tell Right from Wrong* (New York: Simon & Schuster, 1992), which, as they point out, contains a 45-page annotated bibliography of great books for kids of all ages.

In every culture stories are told to impress children with the consequences of their actions. A Caribbean book by Wendy Lohse, which is lushly illustrated by Jenny Sands, *Is It True, Grandfather?* (London and Basingstoke: Macmillan Education LTD, 1996), demonstrates the concern of all when children get lost. *Nathaniel Talking* is a rap, blues, and free verse poetry book written from a Black nine-year old's perspective that has won the Coretta Scott King Award for outstanding illustrations, the Honor Book Award for text, and that was designated as an American Library Association Notable Children's Book for 1989. In the book, author Eloise Greenfield and illustrator Jan Spivey Gilchrist have Nathaniel share insights into his sadness over the death of his mother as well as thoughts on happier aspects of his life. (New York, Writers and Readers Publishing Inc., 1993). The same author/illustrator team addresses the love of a son for his father in *First Pink Light* (1991), and a daughter's love and understanding that her world and relationship to her mother will change, in *Indigo and Moonlight Gold* (1991). Disappointment due to family circumstances is a subject presented by many books, each rich with discussion points. Here are three more that have added cultural value: On the subject of not finding time for each other—by Irene Smalls, *Dawn and the Round To-It* (New York: Simon & Schuster Books for Young Readers, 1994) (ages 4–7); relocation away from traditional (Muslim) celebrations and friends—by Rachna Gilmore, *Lights for Gita* (Toronto, Canada: Second Story Press, 1994) (ages 6–9); being adopted into an American family away from home (Korea)—by Allen Say, *Allison* (New York: Houghton Mifflin, 1997) (ages 6–9). To find books and other media that address racial *prejudice*, we recommend you connect with the following publishers and organizations:

Network of Educators on the Americas (NECA): "A national nonprofit organization that works with school communities to develop and promote teaching methods and resources for social and economic justice in the Americas. These projects reflect NECA's goal of promoting peace, justice, and human rights through critical, anti-racist, multicultural education." NECA offers their *Teaching for Change Catalog*: Resources for K–12 Anti-racist, Multicultural Education, P.O. Box 73038, Washington, DC 20056-3038. 202-806-7277. http://www.cldc.howard.edu/-neca/.

The Southern Poverty Law Center: "A non-profit legal and educational foundation." *Teaching Tolerance*, a four-color magazine mailed twice a year at no charge to educators, is published by the Southern Poverty Law Center, 400 Washington Avenue, Montgomery, Alabama 36104. 334-264-0286. Teaching Tolerance Institute: Begun as a three-week training program for thirty K–12 teachers in the summer of 1997. Fax: 334-264-3121.

Knowledge Unlimited®, Inc., P.O. Box 52, Madison, WI 53701. Publisher of a book written by Barbara K. Curry and James Michael Brodie, illustrated by Jerry Butler, *Sweet Words So Brave: The Story of African American Literature.* Described by the *Washington Post Book World:* "This is a sweeping and ambitious book, intended to introduce young children to the giants of African American literature. ... And maybe, just maybe, they'll be inspired enough to become the storytellers of their generation."

There are also publishing groups that focus more generally on sensitive children's and parenting issues. Two of these are: Parenting Press: Books for children and the adults who care for them, P.O. Box 75267, Seattle, WA 98125. 1-800-992-6657; and Active Parenting Publishers, 810 Franklin Court, Suite B, Marietta, GA 30067. 1-800-825-0060. You might look to these or other such publishers to prepare yourself to deal with difficult incidents and communication challenges of family life.

We also recommend the Avon books by Adele Faber and Elaine Mazlish, including *Siblings Without Rivalry, Liberated Parents/Liberated Children, How to Talk So Kids Will Listen & Listen So Kids Will Talk, How to Be the Parent You always Wanted to Be,* and an article entitled, *How to Talk So Students Will Listen.* They also have communication-improving books for children. You can subscribe to their free newsletter at "Newsletter," Faber/Mazlish Workshops, LLC, P.O. Box 37, Rye, NY 10580. 1-800-944-8584.

42. The publishers of *Children's Magazine Guide* offer a video on doing periodical research that won the Distinguished Achievement Award for Excellence in Journalism, awarded by the Educational Press Association of America). Call 1-800-521-8110 for information.

43. Brian Jacques, *Tales from Redwall* (series) (New York: Philomel Books, 1986–current).

44. Gary Paulson, (series) (New York: Delacorte Press, 1987–current).

45. C.S. Lewis, *The Chronicles of Narnia* (series) (New York: HarperCollins, 1955).

46. J. K. Rowling, *Harry Potter and the Philosopher's Stone* (a.k.a. *Harry Potter and the Sorcerer's Stone*) (series) (Great Britain: Bloomsbury, 1997–current).

CHAPTER TWENTY-SEVEN

Dealing with the Competition

We would be remiss in our desire to help you in creating communicators if we didn't discuss the *opposition*.

As the electronics of computers, the World Wide Web, and television continue to mingle, you will need to discuss, supervise, and evaluate your children's use of the media. There are so many valid uses for computers, we think rejecting them wholesale is as ludicrous as rejecting cars or public transportation. However, you wouldn't give your car keys to your eight year old, and you would do well to "ride along" on the use of the computer.

Like television or movies, computer game software is filled with images and messages. Some, even if rated, may not be appropriate for *your* children. And with so much violence and hatred being spread through the Web, in the guise of sites of interest to young adults, you would do well to discuss the impact of the media, then keep computers centrally located, rather than in private rooms.

And what about the ever-present electronic baby sitter—the boob tube?

One of us was a TV addict until we unplugged it fifteen years ago. Since then we've started our family literacy business—The Reading Railroad, written this book, and watched the rise of one of our favorite nonprofits, TV-Free America.[47] We recommend you join forces with them, send away for their information booklet, and participate in their yearly National Turn-Off TV week. Without your active participation and supervision, your children will have a difficult time breaking free of TV to find and develop their own love of books—not to mention their creativity and imagination.

Keep this in mind: The average child graduating from high school has spent more time in front of the television than going to school! Chilling, isn't it? What can you do? Take control. Limit the types of programs and number of hours viewed. And most of all, keep finding time to read aloud to foster their love of reading.

According to an early report on Indiana University's *Parents Sharing Books* program (now called *Make Reading Fun!*),[48] one parent's communication with his son improved when they started reading *Dune* together. Here's an excerpt from that report:

> "Tony wasn't an avid reader. He brought home *Dune* when someone recommended that he read it, because he loves science and science fiction. We challenged each other and took turns reading, and talking, about the book. The result was that my son became fascinated with reading books like that," says [Carl B.] Smith, Indiana University professor of education and director of the Family Literacy Center. Smith characterized his [strained] relationship with his son as normal before they began discussing issues such as human beings living on a planet without water, as happened in the world of Dune. "We began talking to each other like human beings," Smith said.

Remember, when you read a book together, you are meeting a character whose ideas and actions you can discuss, enjoy—and learn from—anytime, anywhere. If it seems best, thoughtful discussion can wait until you're having breakfast, or have a moment alone in the car together. Try an opener that invites your child's reflective thought, like, "I was thinking about how (name a character) felt when (name an event). Did you expect (character) to (decision or action)?" Whether it's Maniac McGee[49] facing a racist neighbor, or Winnie the Pooh[50] with a honey pot stuck on his head, there's ample opportunity to explore a feeling wherever you are with your children. If it would help, when you finish reading aloud, make a few notes of issues to discuss when you are alone together at another time.

The report continues:

> At age 12, most kids stop reading, even avid readers. There are more interesting things to do. Some kids stop all together. There is a low literacy performance in our country. Our kids stop reading and others don't," the professor [Smith] says.

Once the staff at the Family Literacy Center at Indiana University decided to tackle this problem by starting a *Parents Sharing Books* program, reports of improved parent/child relationships and reading habits began to come in. One parent admitted that time is a big factor:

> "Usually we let other activities get in the way. We started reading while in the car and while making dinner. Then her father started reading with her. He never did this before and she really enjoys that...."

Becoming a family that values reading aloud together takes a commitment on everyone's part. But there is a final point which needs to be mentioned. We sometimes talk with parents who love books, read to their kids as they are growing up, read for their own pleasure, and still wind up with children who are turned off by books or find reading boring and uninteresting. Admittedly this one stumped us for awhile until we read *Parents Who Love Reading, Kids Who Don't—How It Happens and What You Can Do About It* by Mary Leonhardt.[51] This book is a must read for every parent because Ms. Leonhardt, a high school English teacher in Massachusetts, has written a clear, fun-to-read book filled with practical experience and ideas about how to combat some of the turn-offs to infusing a love of reading in children.

You, as parents, can make a difference in your children's lives and love of literacy, at any point in time. Read the resources, talk it over, try it out—and enjoy a lifetime of benefits!

Check it out!

47. TV-Free America is a national nonprofit organization that encourages Americans to reduce, voluntarily and dramatically, the amount of television they watch in order to promaote richer, healthier and more connected lives, families and communities. To learn how to organize a local TV-Turnoff in your school, library or community, contact: TV-Free America, 1611 Connecticut Avenue N.W., Suite 3A, Washington, DC, 20009 Tel: 202-887-0436, www.essential.org/orgs/tvfa.

48. Formerly, the *Parents Sharing Books* Program. With *Make Reading Fun!* parents and children of all levels Pre-K–9 learn how to share the same book by talking about it and relating their feelings and ideas to each other. They learn to identify their mutual interests, select books together, and use a variety of strategies for sharing—such as drawing, writing, and informal drama—in addition to reading aloud and book conversations. For more information about programs currently offered in your area, or to learn how to become a leader for groups of parents in your community (materials available in Spanish and English), call Ellie Macfarlane at 1-888-326-5488.

49. Jerry Spinelli, *Maniac Magee* (New York: Little, Brown and Company, Inc., 1990).

50. A.A. Milne, *The World of Pooh* (E.P. Dutton & Company, Inc., 1957).

51. Mary Leonhardt, *Parents Who Love Reading, Kids Who Don't—How It Happens and What You Can Do About It* (Three Rivers Press, 1995).

AFTERWORD

Reading Aloud in Families:
Where do you go from here?

The shameful period of our nation's history characterized by the slave trade was, in part, supported and perpetuated by the rule: *slaves are not to be taught to read or write.* Slave owners contended that a slave no longer made a *good* slave once he or she became literate.

Unlock the mind and imagination of a people by putting the power to read and write into their hands and they rise up to throw off their shackles and demand their right to "life, liberty, and the pursuit of happiness."

That's a powerful endorsement of literacy and of fostering the love of literature in today's children, but where does it all lead? Once you and your children are in the habit of reading aloud and talking about the plots and characters and actions in children's books, and your kids are getting old enough to comfortably read to themselves, what's next?

First, get yourself a copy of Jim Trelease's book, *Read All About It! Great Read-Aloud Stories, Poems, & Newspaper Pieces for Preteens and Teens.*[52] It's a collection of great read-aloud pieces, which will help point kids in the right direction as their taste in literature matures. Just as they'll finally outgrow their love of cotton candy, they'll also become ready for "meatier" literature to feed their inquisitive minds.

As your kids get older, you will all participate in family discussions about some of the knottier problems that they're facing in school, with friends, and those that they read about in the newspaper or see on TV. But realize that once you and your kids have begun using books to help them voice their young concerns, children's literature can continue to open up dialogues about some of the tougher moral issues they face. Why, for eons good storytellers have been wrapping thorny ethical problems in even simple folk tales, or fables, to foster thinking.

Let's go on a journey back in time to talk with one of the early storytellers. Here we go, step into our time machine—dial in 2,600 years ago. Around 600 B.C. And, let's set the location for Greece. We're going to talk with a Greek fabulist.

While the machine is taking us back we'll tell you what a fabulist is— it's a person who writes fables. Any idea who we might be dropping in to see? A feisty but good-hearted old gent named Æsop. You know, that author who wrote those funny tales some of us learned as children: *The Tortoise and the Hare*, *The Boy Who Cried Wolf*, *The Fox and the Grapes*.

We won't bother him for very long.

"Excuse us … Mr. Æsop?"

"Come on in youngsters … it's good to see you … but I can't give you much time."

"Just a few questions, Mr. Æsop—we're here to ask you why you wrote all those kids' fairy tales … those fables … *The Tortoise and the Hare*, *The Fox and the Grapes*?"

"What're you young'uns, a bunch of ninnies? Fairy tales! Kids fables! You never heard of censorship?"

"Well, yeah, but what has that got to do with it?"

"WHAT HAS THAT GOT TO DO WITH IT? Let me tell you what that's got to do with it! You take a universal truth, and if you speak it outright or write it down, you wind up in leg irons and living on gruel. Dictators don't like the masses to be educated, you know … stupid and uneducated is much easier to control. But, those universal truths … *they've got to be told!* The next generation needs them as much as we do. So I take a truth and wrap it in an allegory with a bunch of animals. A rabbit here, a turtle there, a fox and some grapes … and voilà … I don't hurt anybody's political feelings and the message gets passed along.

"Now leave me to my work. I've got to finish the fable I'm writing now. Ah! Look at that sundial! I gotta get down to the toga cleaners before they close today and I've miles to go before I sleep."

"Gee, we didn't know you wrote that!"

Of course I wrote it—I'm thinking of calling it the 'Sparrow that Laid the Golden Egg ...'"

"I meant ... never mind. What if you called it the '*Goose* that Laid the Golden Egg?'"

"Hmm, that's got a nice ring to it ... I'll think about it. Good day!"

As we leave Æsop to pick up his toga and debate about the title of his newest fable, think back to how *you* first learned about those universal truths that all of us should think about, make our own, and pass on to the next generation.

Remember the day your parents took you aside and said, "OK, we should sit down and have a little talk about honesty, fairness, courage, justice, compassion, truth, and love"? Probably not! Most likely it never took place. And why is that? Isn't it in part because it's so hard to discuss those moral values in a vacuum? But that's where Æsop's fables and other fine literature come in. As a parent it's much easier to use a parable, and children find it much easier to remember the concepts from a story than a long dissertation.

Often after ideas are delivered in tales about rabbits and tortoises and foxes and crows, children themselves bring them into play when a family member needs the encouragement that "slow and steady wins the race," or a reminder that "pride goes before a fall."

Reading aloud, you can share and discuss literature that illustrates truth or kindness or fairness.

And you don't need to consider *yourself* exceptionally wise and eloquent in order to give your children these universal ideas. You can simply be wise enough to use books, discussion, and your love of reading and language to foster your children's moral growth. This will help them in their own lives at home, at school, and in the community.

Good literature is even being used to help stop kids from going down the path to self-destruction and violence. In fact, it can literally keep them out of jail! The state of Massachusetts has an innovative alternative program for frequent offenders facing jail. The program, put together by a District Court judge and a professor from the University of Massachusetts at Dartmouth, sentences convicts to read, study, and discuss good literature.

The program is working—decreasing recidivism by almost two and a half times the normal rate. Through literature, repeat offenders are given the opportunity to acquire the training of mind and heart that enables them to better deal with issues of morality, justice, and fairness in their own lives. Discussing how characters in a book deal with challenges similar to their own, they begin to see how to deal with problems by thinking and talking, not using their fists!

Together, while your children are still at home, you and literature can feed their hearts and minds to get them started on the pathway to moral, fulfilling lives. As Jim Trelease likes to say: "Fifteen minutes a day can make an incredible difference in the life of a child."

Fifteen minutes a day—

• Of you and *Alice in Wonderland:*[53] "Alice was beginning to get very tired of sitting by her sister on the bank, and of having nothing to do; once or twice she had peeped into the book her sister was reading, but it had no pictures or conversations in it, 'and what is the use of a book,' thought Alice, 'without pictures or conversations?'"

• Of you and *Mufaro's Beautiful Daughters:*[54] "A long time ago, in a certain place in Africa, a small village lay across a river and half a day's journey from a city where a great king lived. A man named Mufaro lived in this village with his two daughters, who were called mahn-YAR-ah and nee-AH-sha. Everyone agreed that Manyara and Nyasha were very beautiful."

- Of you and *Maniac Magee:*[55] "They say Maniac Magee was born in a dump. They say his stomach was a cereal box and his heart a sofa spring.... What's true, what's myth? It's hard to know."
- Of you and Harry Potter:[56] "Harry Potter was a highly unusual boy in many ways. For one thing, he hated the summer holidays more than any other time of year. For another, he really wanted to do his homework, but was forced to do it in secret, in the dead of night. And he also happened to be a wizard."

As children learn to talk about and address life's moral issues as introduced in children's stories today, they are becoming the thinkers, communicators, and arbiters who can deal with the complex problems that will face them as caring parents and contributing community members in their world of tomorrow. What more could any parent ask?

Check it out!

52. Jim Trelease, *Read All About It! Great Read-Aloud Stories, Poems, & Newspaper Pieces for Preteens and Teens* (New York: Penguin Books, 1993).

53. Lewis Carroll, *Alice in Wonderland* (Rand McNally & Company, 1916). There is also an aboriginal version of Lewis Carroll's *Alice's Adventures in Wonderland*, adapted and translated by Nancy Sheppard with stunning illustrations by Donna Leslie, called *Alitji in Dreamland*, or *Alitjinya Ngura Tjukurmankuntjala* (Berkeley, CA: Berkeley Press, 1992). First published in Australia (The Department of Adult Education, the University of Adelaide, North Terrace, Adelaide, South Australia 5000). In these editions, the white rabbit is a kangaroo. The opening passage reads:

> Alitji was getting very tired of sitting in the creek bed. She and her sister had been playing milpatjunanyi, a story-telling game. They each had a stick and a pile of leaves, and took it in turn to tell a story about their family. The sandy

ground was their stage; the leaves were the people. As they told the stories, each softly tapped her stick in time to the rhythm of her rising and falling voice, and every now and then they would sweep the sand smooth with the backs of their hands.

Alitji had become very bored as her sister's voice went on and on, and her eyelids began to droop. "Well," she said to herself, "perhaps I'll collect some tjintjulu berries to decorate my hair." ... Suddenly a kangaroo hopped past her saying, "Oh dear, oh deary me, I'm late."

54. John Steptoe, *Mufaro's Beautiful Daughters* (New York: Lothrop, Lee, & Shepard Books, 1987).

55. Jerry Spinelli, *Maniac Magee* (New York: Little, Brown & Company, Inc., 1990).

56. J.K. Rowling, *Harry Potter and the Prisoner of Azkaban* (Scholastic Press, 1999).

APPENDIX I

Performance Reading Practice and Win-Win Word Games Index

PERFORMANCE READING PRACTICE

APPENDIX II

Children's Magazines

What child doesn't love getting mail? After sampling magazines that match your child's interests, which you're sure to find in your local bookstores and libraries, get a subscription. The incentive to read is greatly increased just by having something special come to the house with your child's name on it.

This is not an exhaustive list ... we're aware of over fifty magazines currently aimed at kids. But you'll find numerous magazines published by Cobblestone Publishing Company. We are very impressed with the company and its intent to make information available to students in age-appropriate and contemporary ways, drawing on experts in every field. For a thorough overview of their periodicals and extensive educational services, visit their website <www.cobblestonepub.com>. We hope you'll give them feedback on their magazine line—particularly those specializing in your area of expertise, and Black history for children 9–14.

The age recommendations are only to be used as rough guidelines.

INFANTS (0-2)

Babybug. Published by the editors of *Ladybug, Spider,* and *Cricket.* Think of it as a board book magazine filled with simple rhymes and stories to share again and again with your infant-toddler. 1-800-827-0227.

YOUNG CHILDREN (2-7)

Click. (3-7) Opens up the wonders of the real world. Young explorers will learn fascinating details about the arts, sciences, cultures, history, nature and the environment through stories, exposition, activities, and art. It's published by the team that brings you *Ladybug, Spider, Muse,* et al. Guidance for parents. 1-800-827-0227.

Ladybug. (2-6) Full of colorful drawings, songs, poems, games, and author interviews. Includes helpful ideas for interactive reading. 1-800-827-0227.

Your Big Back Yard. Published by the National Wildlife Federation. It focuses on conservation and environmental issues for preschoolers. 1-800-611-1599.

Sesame Street. An opportunity to make TV work for you! Number games, stories, poems, and color-ins based on "Sesame Street" characters. When you subscribe you receive a special parents' guide with your child's magazine. 1-800-678-0613.

CHILDREN (6-9)

American Girl Magazine. A magazine that's busy and buzzing with feelings, jokes, facts about friendships, and famous and not-so-famous American girls. Reader response feeds problem-solving discussion with can-do-it answers. 1-800-234-1278.

Appleseeds. Quality articles, interviews, and stories colorfully presented with fascinating photographs and original illustrations. You'll find activities and games that develop skills and interest in geography, history, vocabulary, math, and science. The editors say, "*Appleseeds* plants the seed of a love of reading." Cobblestone Publishing Company: 1-800-821-0115.

Ranger Rick. Marvelously corny riddles, an advice column—"Ask Hoppy," stories, informative articles, excellent photography, and letters from kids. Published by the editors of *Your Big Back Yard.* 1-800-611-1599.

Spider. A charming collection of the best stories, poems, songs, games, and adventures for young children by the publishers of *Click*, *Babybug*, and *Ladybug*. Includes special activity inserts and help for parents. 1-800-827-0227.

Boy's Life. Role models for boys in adventure stories and cartoons, by the Boy Scouts of America, Box 152079, Irving, TX, 75015. 1-214-580-2000

Highlights for Children. A staple for generations, including stories, picture puzzles, and games. Highlights for Children, Inc., Box 269, Columbus Ohio, 43216. 1-614-486-0631.

Sports Illustrated for Kids. For the girl and boy sports fans in your household. 1-800-336-0116.

Boys' Quest. (6-13) No teenage themes. No advertising. A wide variety of stories and how-to activities on a monthly theme. 1-800-358-4732.

OLDER CHILDREN (9-14)

Note: *Children's Magazine Guide* is a manageable bimonthly periodical guide for children, indexing a broad cross-section of articles from children's magazines. An award-winning training video to teach children how to use a periodical guide to literature is available. 1-800-521-8110.

Cobblestone. Published during the nine months of the school year, this magazine challenges students to think. The editors describe their means as thoughtful articles and discussions that encourage students to react with, "Wow! I didn't know that!" Content includes primary documents, historical photographs, contests, and lively historically accurate articles. Cobblestone Publishing Company: 1-800-821-0115.

California Chronicles. Along with an opportunity to have California-related questions answered by experts, the editors promise "a guided tour of the most exciting moments in California's history. " Look for themed issues covering geography, literature, art, and science presented with games and puzzles. Cobblestone Publishing Company: 1-800-821-0115.

Cricket. The next step up from *Spider,* and an engaging magazine that *you'll* probably peruse. 1-800-827-0227.

Calliope. World History for young people. Cultural strengths, mysteries, and traditions are examined in the light of their influence on people then and now, there and here. Intriguing archaeological reports, non-fiction essays, and quizzes. Cobblestone Publishing Company: 1-800-821-0115.

Footsteps. This African-American history magazine illustrates and honors the history and achievements of people of African descent. Expect non-fiction accounts, art, crafts, recipes, maps, time lines, and more. Cobblestone Publishing Company: 1-800-821-0115.

National Geographic World. The official magazine for junior members of the National Geographic Society. 1-800-647-5463.

Muse. From the publishers of *Cricket* and *Smithsonian* magazines, *Muse* is much like the Smithsonian in its vast coverage of the arts, sciences, and humanities. Includes humor, sidebars, and photos in contemporary layouts; publishes readers; runs contests; and offers website contact information to those interested in doing scientific research. 1-800-827-0227.

Odyssey. Garnering the Parents' Choice Award, this 49-page award-winning physical science, astronomy, and space science magazine features articles, "Science Scoops," interviews with scientists, spectacular photographs and illustrations, and hands-on activities so home or classroom readers can *do* science. Cobblestone Publishing Company: 1-800-821-0115.

Skipping Stones. A multicultural children's magazine. If your children are interested in other cultures and kids from "far off lands," *Skipping Stones* will delight them. The editors state: "We especially encourage submissions by youth from under-represented populations." Additionally they say: "(We are) designed to expand horizons in a playful, creative way." They do just that. 1-514-342-4956.

Faces. Anthropologists and archaeologists introduce the world's cultures. Readers can try their recipes, play their games. Includes articles, activities, first-hand accounts, folktales, legends, and letters page. Parents' Choice Award and EDPRESS Achievement Award. Supports National Geography Standards for education. Cobblestone Publishing Company: 1-800-821-0115.

The Wild Outdoor World. A magazine for "young conservationists." Substantial environmental magazine to help children get involved and make a difference. Crisp writing and full-color photos. Published by the Rocky Mountain Elk Foundation, 1-888 301-5437.

Girls' Life. Girls will enjoy the many interviews that give the inside scoop on what others (including boys) are thinking about issues that concern them. 1-888-999-3222.

Zillions is published by Consumers Union, the same group that puts out *Consumer Reports*. It's published six times a year as an advertising-free magazine, which has won many awards including EdPress Distinguished Achievement Awards for excellence in educational journalism. There is no toll-free number for subscriptions but you can write to them at Zillions Subscription Department P.O. Box 5177, Boulder, CO 80323-1777. If you or your child doesn't like it they'll refund your money on all unmailed issues.

Cicada. Something new for teenagers and young adults, from the publishers of *Cricket*. Full of beautiful art, fun, and stories.1-800-827-0227.

CHILDREN'S MAGAZINES MAINLY BY CHILDREN

The Children's Magazine. Thoughtful reflections by children, both as stories and poetry. Professionally illustrated. Contributors identified by photo, age, grade, and geographic location. Classroom submissions encouraged. 602-483-2100.

Stone Soup. By children, for children. Art, book reviews, stories and poems all from children up to the age of 13. You'll love it too! 1-800-447-4569.

New Moon: the magazine for girls and their dreams. An international magazine for girls ages 8–14. Submissions cover science, culture, history, and the unique challenges facing girls growing up. 1-800-381-4743.

APPENDIX III

Check It Out! Summary of Chapter Notes

P lease notice that the first references to resources occur in CHAPTER 13, and that they do not occur in every chapter. For a more detailed description and recommendation of many of the following resources, see **Check it out!** at the close of each chapter indicated below:

CHAPTER 13

James Gurney, *Dinotopia* (Atlanta: Turner Publishing, Inc., 1992); *Dinotopia: The World Beneath* (1995); and *Dinotopia: First Flight* (New York: HarperCollins Publishers, 1999).

CHAPTER 14

John Dolman, Jr., *The Art of Reading Aloud* (New York: Harper & Brothers, 1956).

Jessica Somers Driver, *Speak for Yourself* (Jessica Somers Driver, 1948).

Nedra Newkirk Lamar, *How to Speak the Written Word* (Old Tappan, New Jersey: Fleming H. Revell Company, 1967).

CHAPTER 17

Beth Hilgartner, *Great Gorilla Grins: An Abundance of Alliterations* (Boston: Little, Brown, 1979).

Steven Kellogg, *Aster Aardvark's Alphabet Adventures* (New York: Morrow, 1987).

Maurice Sendak, *Alligators All Around: An Alphabet—An alligator jamboree with all letters, A through Z* (New York: HarperCollins, 1962).

Stan Berenstain, *The Berenstain Bears and Queenie's Crazy Crush* (New York: Random House, 1997).

Chapter 18

Robert Claiborne, *Loose Cannons & Red Herrings: A book of lost metaphors* (New York: Penguin Books, 1988).

Robert A. Palmatier, *Speaking of Animals: a dictionary of animal metaphors* (Westport, CT: Greenwood Press, 1995).

Chapter 19

Bill Martin, Jr. and John Archambault, *Chicka Chicka Boom Boom* (New York: Simon and Schuster, Inc., 1989).

Chapter 24

Charge of the Light Brigade, by Alfred Tennyson

Richard Cory, by Edwin A. Robinson

The Highwayman, by Alfred Noyes

From Sea to Shining Sea, A Treasury of American Folklore and Folk Songs, compiled by Amy L. Cohn (New York: Scholastic, Inc., 1993).

Celebrate America in Poetry and Art, edited by Nora Panzer (New York: Hyperion Books for Children, 1994).

Katharine Lee Bates, with art by Wayne Thiebaud, *O Beautiful for Spacious Skies* (San Francisco: Chronicle Books, 1994). Edited by Sara Jane Boyers.

How Sweet the Sound: African-American Songs for Children, songs selected by Wade and Cheryl Hudson with illustrations by Floyd Cooper (New York: Scholastic, Inc., 1995).

Chapter 25

Patton Tabors, research coordinator of The Home-School Study. *Harvard Education Letter*, 1997, Vol. 13, No. 4, page 2.

Journal of Research in Childhood Education 1991, Vol. 6, No. 1, page 30. David K. Dickinson, Clark University and Patton O. Tabors, Harvard Graduate School of Education. Copyright 1991 by the Association for Childhood Education International 0256-8543/91.

Dorothy Kunhardt, *Pat the Bunny* (New York: Western Publishing Company, Inc., 1942).

Jack Hanna, *The Petting Zoo* (New York: Doubleday, 1992).

English translation by Yvonne Hooker, *Wheels Go Round*, (New York: Grosset & Dunlap, 1990).

Richard Scarry (series) (New York: Random House).

Dick Witt, *Let's Look at Animals* (New York: Scholastic, 1993).

Willi Baum, *The Expedition* (Glasgow and London: Blackie, 1976).

Jim Trelease, *Hey! Listen to This: Stories to Read Aloud* (New York: Penguin Books, 1992), page 8.

Board Books:

Satoshi Kitamara, *Duck is Dirty* (New York: Farrar, Straus, & Giroux, 1996). First published in Great Britain by Andersen Press, 1996).

Eloise Greenfield, with illustrations by Jan Spivey Gilchrist, *Aaron and Gayla's Counting Book* (New York: Black Butterfly Children's Books by Writers and Readers Publishing Inc., 1993).

Picture books:

Ezra Jack Keats, *The Snowy Day* (New York: Puffin Books, 1962).

Marie Hall Ets, *Gilberto and the Wind* (also Puffin, 1978).

Æsop, *The Sun and the Wind*.

Martin Handford, *Where's Waldo?* (Cambridge: Candlewick Press, 1997).

Arthur Dorros, *Abuela* (New York: Dutton Children's Books, 1991); also *Isla*, 1995.

Lucy Micklethwait, *I Spy a Freight Train: Transportation in Art* (New York: Greenwillow Books, 1996).

Graeme Base, *Animalia* (New York: Harry N. Abrams, Inc., 1986).

Joan Steiner, *Look Alikes* (Boston: Little, Brown & Company, 1998).

Jane Yolen, *Owl Moon* (New York: Philomel Books, 1987).

Esphyr Slobodkina, *Caps for Sale: A tale of a peddler, some monkeys, and their monkey business* (New York: HarperCollins, 1984).

Shel Silverstein's poetry and drawings: *Where the Sidewalk Ends* (New York: HarperCollins, 1974), *A Light in the Attic* (New York: HarperCollins, 1981), and *Falling Up* (New York: HarperCollins, 1996). Also look for his stories: *The Giving Tree* (New York: Harper & Row, 1964), and *The Missing Piece Meets the Big O* (New York: HarperCollins, 1981).

American Girls Collection (Middleton, WI: Pleasant Co.). Over twenty books by several authors.

Sharon A. Edwards and Robert W. Maloy, *Kids Have All The Write Stuff, Inspiring Your Children to Put Pencil (or crayon or felt-tip marker or computer) to Paper* (New York: Penguin Books, Inc., 1992).

Chris Van Allsburg, *The Mysteries of Harris Burdick* (Boston: Houghton Mifflin Company, 1984).

CHAPTER 26

Francelia Butler, *Sharing Literature with Children* (New York: Longman, Inc., 1977).

Lucy Calkins, *Raising Lifelong Learners, A Parent's Guide* (Reading, MA: Addison-Wesley, 1997)

Bernice Cullinan, *Read to Me: Raising Kids Who Love to Read* (New York: Scholastic, 1992).

Ask for the latest update of this book: Eden Ross Lipson, *The New York Times Parent's Guide to the Best Books for Children* (New York: Times Books, 1988).

Jim Trelease, *Hey! Listen to This: Stories to Read Aloud* (New York: Penguin Books, 1992).

Kathleen Odean, *Great Books for Girls* (Ballantine, 1997) and *Great Books for Boys* (Ballentine, 1998).

Anansi Finds a Fool: An Ashanti Tale (New York: Dial Books for Young Readers, 1992), from *Akan-Ashanti Folk Tales* (Oxford: Clarendon Press, 1930).

As retold by Eric A. Kimmel, *Anansi and the Moss-Covered Rock* (New York: Holiday House, 1988).

Dr. Thomas Lickona, *Raising Good Children* (New York: Bantam Books, 1994), which includes these recommendations:

The Heartwood Ethics Curriculum for Children: Heartwood Institute, 12300 Perry Highway, Wexford, PA 15090; 412-934-1777).

Elizabeth Baird Saenger, *Exploring Ethics Through Children's Literature* (Critical Thinking Press and Software, P.O. Box 448, Pacific Grove, CA 93950-0448).

William Kilpatrick, *Why Johnny Can't Tell Right from Wrong* (New York: Simon & Schuster, 1992).

Wendy Lohse, with illustrations by Jenny Sands, *Is It True, Grandfather?* (London and Basingstoke: MacMillan Education LTD, 1996).

Eloise Greenfield, with illustrations by Jan Spivey Gilchrist, *Nathaniel Talking* (New York, Writers and Readers Publishing Inc., 1993).
—*First Pink Light* (1991).
—*Indigo and Moonlight Gold* (1991).

Irene Smalls, *Dawn and the Round To-It* (New York: Simon & Schuster Books for Young Readers, 1994).

Rachna Gilmore, *Lights for Gita* (Toronto, Canada: Second Story Press, 1994).

Allen Say, *Allison* (New York: Houghten Mifflin, 1997).

To find books and other media that address racial *prejudice*, we recommend you connect with the following publishers and organizations:

Network of Educators on the Americas (NECA): "A national nonprofit organization that works with school communities to develop and promote teaching methods and resources for social and economic justice in the Americas. These projects reflect NECA's goal of promoting peace, justice, and human rights through critical, anti-racist, multicultural education." NECA offers their *Teaching for Change Catalog*: Resources for K–12 Anti-racist, Multicultural Education, P.O. Box 73038, Washington, DC 20056-3038. 202-806-7277. <www.teachingforchange.org>.

The Southern Poverty Law Center: "A non-profit legal and educational foundation." *Teaching Tolerance*, a four-color magazine mailed twice a year at no charge to educators, is published by The Southern Poverty Law Center, 400 Washington Avenue, Montgomery, Alabama 36104. 334-264-0286.

Teaching Tolerance Institute: Begun as a three-week training program for thirty K–12 teachers in the summer of 1997. Fax: 334-264-3121.

Knowledge Unlimited®, Inc., P.O. Box 52, Madison, WI 53701. Publisher of a book written by Barbara K. Curry and James Michael Brodie, illustrated by Jerry Butler, *Sweet Words So Brave: The Story of African American Literature*. Described by the *Washington Post*

Book World: "This is a sweeping and ambitious book, intended to introduce young children to the giants of African American literature. ... And maybe, just maybe, they'll be inspired enough to become the storytellers of their generation."

There are also publishing groups that focus more generally on sensitive children's and parenting issues. Three of these are:

Parenting Press: Books for children and the adults who care for them. P.O. Box 75267, Seattle, WA 98125. 1-800-992-6657.
Active Parenting Publishers, 810 Franklin Court, Suite B, Marietta, GA 30067. 1-800-825-0060.
Adele Faber and Elaine Mazlish, *How to Talk So Kids Will Listen & Listen So Kids Will Talk,* (New York: Avon Books, 1980)
  – *Liberated Parents/Liberated Children*
  – *Siblings Without Rivalry*
  – *How to Be the Parent You always Wanted to Be*
Faber and Mazlish also have communication-improving books for children. You can subscribe to their free newsletter at "Newsletter," Faber/Mazlish Workshops, LLC, P.O. Box 37, Rye, NY 10580. 1-800-944-8584.

The publisher of *Children's Magazine Guide,* R.R. Bowker, offers a video on doing periodical research that won the Distinguished Achievement Award for Excellence in Educational Journalism, awarded by the Educational Press Association of America. Call 1-800-521-8110 for information.
Brian Jacques, *Tales from Redwall* (series) (New York: Philomel Books, 1986–).
Gary Paulson, *Hatchet* (series) (New York: Delacorte Press, 1999).
C.S. Lewis, *The Chronicles of Narnia* (New York: HarperCollins, 1955).
J. K. Rowling, *Harry Potter and the Philosopher's Stone* (a.k.a. *Harry Potter and the Sorcerer's Stone* (series)(Great Britain: Bloomsbury, 1997–).

CHAPTER 27

TV-Free America is a national nonprofit organization that encourages Americans to reduce, voluntarily and dramatically, the amount of television they watch in order to promaote richer, healthier and more connected lives, families and communities. To learn how to organize a local TV-Turnoff in your school, library or community, contact: TV-Free America, 1611 Connecticut Avenue N.W., Suite 3A, Washington, DC, 20009 Tel: 202-887-0436, www.essential.org/orgs/tvfa.

Make Reading Fun! Formerly, the *Parents Sharing Books* Program. Call Ellie Macfarlane at 1-888-326-5488.

Jerry Spinelli, *Maniac Magee* (New York: Little, Brown & Company, Inc., 1990).

A.A. Milne, *The World of Pooh* (E.P. Dutton & Company, Inc., 1957).

Mary Leonhardt, *Parents Who Love Reading, Kids Who Don't—How It Happens and What You Can Do About It* (Three Rivers Press, 1995).

AFTERWORD

Jim Trelease, *Read All About It! Great Read-Aloud Stories, Poems, & Newspaper Pieces for Preteens and Teens* (New York: Penguin Books, 1993).

An aboriginal version of Lewis Carroll's *Alice in Wonderland* (Rand McNally & Company, 1916), was adapted and translated by Nancy Sheppard, with illustrations by Donna Leslie, *Alitji in Dreamland*, or *Alitjinya Ngura Tjukurmankuntjala* (Berkeley, California: Berkeley Press, 1992). First published in Australia (The Department of Adult Education, The University of Adelaide, North Terrace, Adelaide, South Australia 5000.)

John Steptoe, *Mufaro's Beautiful Daughters* (New York: Lothrop, Lee, & Shepard Books, 1987).

Jerry Spinelli, *Maniac Magee* (New York: Little, Brown & Company, Inc., 1990).

J.K. Rowling, *Harry Potter and the Prisoner of Azkaban* (Scholastic Press, 1999).

NOTES

Now it's your turn.

We would love to hear about your hopes and dreams and practical steps toward a more literate nation and your interest in community-wide performance reading.

In fact, we want you to hear from each other as well, through our publications and website. Let us know how you're working to improve literacy, and what you've enjoyed sharing from *Read it Aloud!* with your family and community. Tell us your insights, and please let us know if you would like to submit original stories or poems for publication on our website.

For more information about submissions and publications, you can call us toll-free at 1-888-875-5368. You can visit our website at <www.reading-railroad.com>. Or you can drop us a note at:

The Reading Railroad
Read it Aloud!
14 Woodland Street
Natick, MA 01760-5414

Read it Aloud!

– A book that's loved by those who teach reading and will teach those who love reading!

A parent's guide to sharing books with young children

Name: _____

Address: _____

City: _____ State: _____ Zip: _____

Telephone: _____

e-mail address: _____

Mail this form to:
BookMasters, Inc.
P.O. Box 388
Ashland, OH 44805

Read it Aloud! A parent's guide to sharing books with young children $19.95.
Quantity Discount: Take $3.99 off two books!

Quantity (   ) x 19.95/book: _____
10% quantity discount: _____
Subtotal _____
Sales tax on books to _____
❏ MA 5% ❏ OH 6.25%
Subtotal _____
Shipping: (US) _____
$4.95 first book and
$2.50 for each additional book.
Total Payment: _____

(For larger orders, please call the toll-free number below.)

Or call BookMasters toll free:
1-800-247-6553
Fax Orders: 419-281-6883
Online: reading-railroad.com
[e-mail: order@bookmaster.com]

❏ Check   ❏ Credit Card: ❏ Visa ❏ MasterCard ❏ AMEX ❏ Discover

Card number: _____

Exp.date: _____ / _____

Name on card _____

1e-001

Read it Aloud!

– A book that's loved by those who teach reading and will teach those who love reading!

A parent's guide to sharing books with young children

Name: _____

Address: _____

City: _____ State: _____ Zip: _____

Telephone: _____

e-mail address: _____

Mail this form to:
BookMasters, Inc.
P.O. Box 388
Ashland, OH 44805

Read it Aloud! A parent's guide to sharing books with young children $19.95.
Quantity Discount: Take $3.99 off two books!

Quantity ( ) x 19.95/book: _____
10% quantity discount: _____
Subtotal _____
Sales tax on books to _____
❏ MA 5% ❏ OH 6.25%
Subtotal _____
Shipping: (US) _____
$4.95 first book and
$2.50 for each additional book.
Total Payment: _____

(For larger orders, please call the toll-free number below.)

Or call BookMasters toll free:
1-800-247-6553
Fax Orders: 419-281-6883
Online: reading-railroad.com
[e-mail: order@bookmaster.com]

❏ Check   ❏ Credit Card: ❏ Visa ❏ MasterCard ❏ AMEX ❏ Discover

Card number: _____

Exp.date: _____ / _____

Name on card _____

1e-001

Read it Aloud!

– A book that's loved by those who teach reading and will teach those who love reading!

A parent's guide to sharing books with young children

Name: _____

Address: _____

City: _____ State: _____ Zip: _____

Telephone: _____

e-mail address: _____

Mail this form to:
BookMasters, Inc.
P.O. Box 388
Ashland, OH 44805

Read it Aloud! A parent's guide to sharing books with young children $19.95.
Quantity Discount: Take $3.99 off two books!

Quantity (   ) x 19.95/book: _____

10% quantity discount: _____

Subtotal   _____

Sales tax on books to   _____
❏ MA 5%   ❏ OH 6.25%

Subtotal   _____

Shipping: (US)   _____
$4.95 first book and
$2.50 for each additional book.

Total Payment: _____

(For larger orders, please call the toll-free number below.)

Or call BookMasters toll free:
1-800-247-6553
Fax Orders: 419-281-6883
Online: reading-railroad.com
[e-mail: order@bookmaster.com]

❏ Check   ❏ Credit Card: ❏ Visa   ❏ MasterCard   ❏ AMEX   ❏ Discover

Card number: _____

Exp.date: _____ / _____

Name on card _____

1e-001